Popular Mechanics

THE GIRL MECHANIC
GOES OUTDOORS

Popular Mechanics

THE GIRL MECHANIC GOES OUTDOORS

160 EXCITING PROJECTS
to MAKE *and* DO

HEARST BOOKS

A division of Sterling Publishing Co., Inc.

New York / London

www.sterlingpublishing.com

CONTENTS

FOREWORD

In this digital era, it is all too easy for girls, young or all grown up, to find themselves indoors, 24/7, instant messaging, chatting on mobile devices, or otherwise plugged into home entertainment systems. Of course, these gadgets have their place. But this book invites adventuresome lasses to set those gadgets aside and step outside into that nearly forgotten wonder that is the great outdoors.

Through nostalgia-filled projects and still-relevant tips, this little volume celebrates a time when people were in touch with the simpler pleasures the outdoors has to offer. For starters, you'll see that the backyard offers ample opportunities for outdoor fun. With a little effort, you and your siblings will be walking on stilts, swinging from a trapeze, or flying a parachute kite in no time.

In fact, if Mom and Dad are handy, girls can enjoy an entire carnival in the backyard, complete with a pirate-ship sandbox, sailing merry-go-round, and even a kid-sized roller coaster. A scooter, roller skates, and seesaw round out the fun.

In addition to these high-spirited outdoor entertainments, this book shares lots of quiet ways to enjoy the natural world. If you've always wanted a playhouse—even one in a tree!—instructions are provided. Perhaps you want to start a garden—our umbrella basket and pint-sized garden tools will set you on the path. Or maybe you are more interested in whipping up a simple hammock to lounge in as you observe your feathered friends enjoying the bird feeder you made from mixing bowls? For every girl of any age who wants to get off the couch and into the backyard, *The Girl Mechanic Goes Outdoors* offers plenty of amusements to keep her happily occupied.

If a camping trip is in your near future, or you've been angling for a chance to go fishing or paddle a canoe, this book will help you hear the call of the wild, whether you're a certified Brownie or well past your Girl Scout days. You may be amused by the ingenuity and thrift of some of the gadgets constructed by yesterday's adventurer; and it's true, the projects, which range from a popcorn popper made from an old coffee can to a homemade smokehouse for preserving the catch of the day to do-it-yourself water wings, are eccentric. But ultimately you are sure to be inspired by these clever tools, which made for successful camping, boating, and fishing trips long before sporting goods manufacturers began marketing fancy gear to the masses.

When the weather turns chilly, snow bunnies of all ages will delight in the many devices this book offers for slipping and sliding in the snow.

Simple instructions make a handsled built from pipe or a bicycle outfitted with runners for the snow all easily within reach. And when those gadgets have run their course, enterprising girls can cozy up in their very own snow house. Or, better still, they can curl up by the fire and make any number of the campfire crafts presented here. Any craft-oriented little girl will enjoy surprising Mom with a handwoven basket or Dad with a hand-braided leather belt. With some assistance, she can even tackle woodworking, crafting little toys or games for the younger children in the household.

By modern standards, the tools and materials available at the time these projects were first published were quite limited, but we are certain you will enjoy this journey into bygone pastimes in the great outdoors. If nothing else, we hope these delightful projects will inspire you to put down that remote control and embark on your own outdoor adventures.

The Editors
Popular Mechanics

CHAPTER 1

BACKYARD AMUSEMENTS

CRUISE AROUND *or* FLY THROUGH *the* AIR

— COASTING IN A SIDEWALK JEEP —

Coasting along easily on veloci-pede ball bearings, this side-walk Jeep will be the pride of any youngster when she or he goes out on "reconnaissance patrols." Being assembled almost entirely of wood, the Jeep can be made with ordinary tools. White pine or other wood that does not warp easily will be satisfactory for the framework. However, the wheels and axle housings should be made of oak or maple or, for each wheel, you can glue together four pieces of ¼-in. hardwood face to face, with the grain running at right angles.

The frame is notched to receive the rear-axle housing, *Figure 2,* after which the front-axle support is drilled and counterbored for the center bolt and doweled to the frame. Next, the front bumper is screwed to the frame, the screw heads being countersunk. To give sufficient strength to the front-axle housing after the pivot hole is drilled, the housing should be made of 1¼-in. stock, *Figure 4,* the bottom edge of the housing being grooved to receive the axle, as shown in *Figure 3.*

Lower edges of the engine hood are doweled and glued to the frame as shown in the lower detail of *Figure 7.* A groove ½ in. wide by ¼ in. deep should be cut on the outside of each piece to receive the top section of the fender, *Figure 5.* The back end of the fender is cut at an angle of 34 degrees, *Figure 6,* the corresponding end of the groove being chiseled to the same angle. The fenders are braced with an iron corner brace, as shown in the upper detail of *Figure 7.* Note that the sloping portion, *Figure 6,* goes under the body

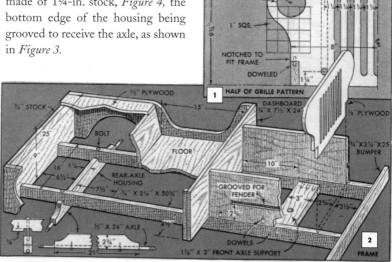

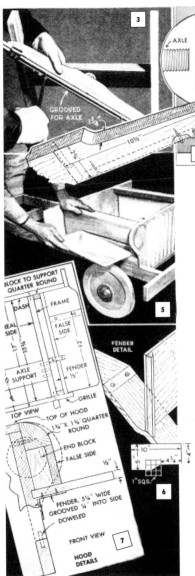

side and that the opposite end is flush with the bottom of the groove cut for the top section of the fender, as shown in *Figure 9.* The horizontal section of the fender is glued into the hood groove and is screwed and glued to the sloping piece.

The grill, dashboard and back are installed as illustrated in *Figures 2* and *9.* The grill is laid out according to the pattern in *Figure 1,* jigsawed as shown, attached to the frame by dowels. Both the grill and the dash are screwed to the ends of the hood, and the back is fastened to the frame with counter-sunk screws. The floor is cut from ½-in. stock, the pieces being butted against the dashboard and nailed to the top of the frame. Before nailing the floor down, however, drill a 1¼-in. hole in the piece adjoining the dashboard, 1¼ in. on center from the front edge, for the steering post.

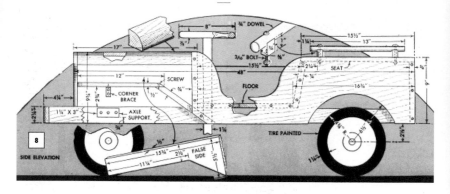

The body sides are 9¾ in. high at the front and 9 in. high at the back, *Figure 8*, with the lower front corner cut off at an angle flush with the fender. The two sides should be tacked together and the curves band-sawed in one operation to assure identical pieces. They are screwed to the back, dashboard, floor, and backrest. The backrest fits behind the floor and extends at an angle to within ½ in. of the top of the sides, both edges being beveled to fit the floor and seat respectively. To make the quarter round used on the sides of the hood, glue four pieces of 2 x 2 x 17-in. wood together, using paper between all joints. Turn this unit to a diameter of 3½ in. and then split it into four quarter-rounds with a chisel. Cut the false engine sides and end blocks shown in *Figure 7*. Making and installing the seat rails will complete the body.

In turning the wheels, a circle 3 in. in diameter should be marked on the wheel with pencil to locate the hub, which will be turned separately. Note that the hole for the bearing is cut partway through the wheel to a point which will allow the bearing to run in the center, as shown in the circular detail, *Figure 4*. Be sure the hole is cut in straight so that the bearing will be tight when it is driven to the center. After the bearing is driven in, it is followed by a tight-fitting wooden collar, glued on. If, however, velocipede bearings are not available, you can turn 1-in. spindles on the ends of an oak axle and drill the wheels to rotate with a snug rather than a binding fit. With this arrangement, spindles must be kept thoroughly lubricated with graphite. To avoid any season cracks, it is well to give the wheel a coat of shellac or sanding sealer immediately after it is

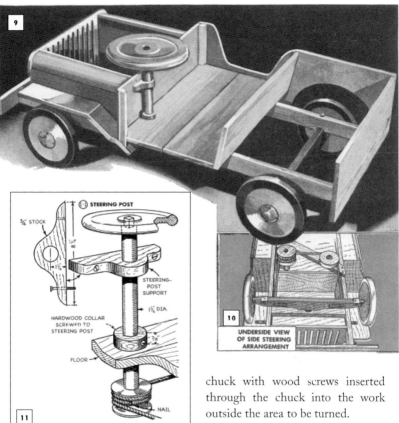

chuck with wood screws inserted through the chuck into the work outside the area to be turned.

The steering wheel and crossarm are glued to their respective ends of the steering post after the support and collar are slipped on and the post is inserted through the floor, as in *Figure 11*. The support is bolted through the dashboard, all bolts being bradded to prevent their working loose. If an all-wood front axle is

finished and sanded. The tire is then painted on with slate-gray porch or deck paint.

A wooden chuck is necessary for turning the hubs. It is merely a 5-in. wooden disk screwed to a 3-in. face plate. The work is fastened to the

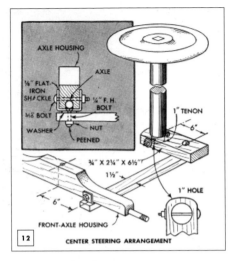

AXLE HOUSING

AXLE

⅛" FLAT-
IRON
SHACKLE

¼" F. H.
BOLT

¼" BOLT

1" TENON

WASHER

NUT

PEENED

6"

¾" X 2¼" X 6½"

1½"

1" HOLE

6"

FRONT-AXLE HOUSING

12 CENTER STEERING ARRANGEMENT

is better to locate these pivot parts when the parts are being assembled to avoid any discrepancies. If two or more youngsters are to ride on the Jeep, the steering wheel may be placed on the left side to allow more than one to ride at the same time. In this case, the steering mechanism will consist of one pulley wide enough to take three turns of the sash cord with a nail through the second turn, and a second pulley over which the cord runs to connect to the axle, as shown in *Figures 10* and *11*. The cord should form perfect right angles when the front axle is square with the frame.

Four sash lifts make the steps on the side of the seat. A floor mat, electric horn and spare wheel are suitable accessories. Paint the body a dull green and use aluminum paint for the headlamps and the star in the middle of the hood.

used, the flat-iron shackles shown in *Figure 4* may be eliminated and the steering rods bolted through both axle and housing, as in *Figure 12*. It is necessary that the steering rods pivot at a point directly beneath the front axle and that they be an equal distance from the center on both the housing and the steering crossarm, otherwise the mechanism will bind when the wheels are turned. It

— SKATE-WHEEL SCOOTER —

This skate-wheel scooter, unlike the usual homemade type, has the steering post pivoted. A block of 2-in. stock supports the steering post, both block and post being slotted to

take a heavy butt-type hinge, which is held in place with stove bolts. The lower end of the steering post and the rear-axle block, both of hardwood, are the same width as the axle

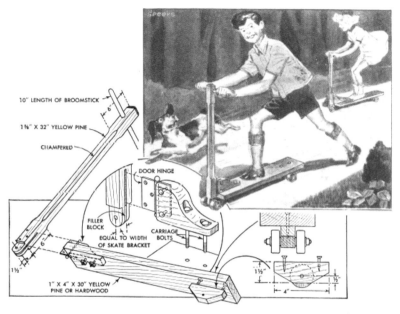

10" LENGTH OF BROOMSTICK

1⅜" X 32" YELLOW PINE

CHAMFERED

DOOR HINGE

FILLER BLOCK

EQUAL TO WIDTH OF SKATE BRACKET

CARRIAGE BOLTS

1½"

1" X 4" X 30" YELLOW PINE OR HARDWOOD

1½"

1½"

4"

supports on the skates, thus making it an easy matter to slip the skate-wheel axles through the holes and attach the wheels. A filler block is used to close the lower end of the slot in the steering post. For the handle, a 10-in. handle of broomstick is inserted in a hole drilled in the steering post and a wood screw is driven in to secure it.

— TIN-CAN STILTS ARE LOTS OF FUN —

Tin-can stilts are inexpensive and safe for children, especially the small tots who want in on the fun. The cans are held on the shoes by rubber bands cut from old inner tubes.

CANS

SPLIT

PIECE OF INNER TUBE

— CHILD'S SWING HAS NO DIAGONAL BRACES ABOVE GROUND —

Bolted securely across two 4 x 4-in. vertical members of a child's swing, a 2-in. plank below the ground surface was found highly effective as a substitute for diagonal bracing, which was desired both on account of the possibility of tripping over the braces and because of its appearance. Side pull exerted on the vertical members is distributed over the entire area of the plank, preventing the vertical members from working loose. All wood underground should be creosoted.

— NON-TIP SWING SEAT FOR YOUNGSTERS —

E

— HOMEMADE ROLLER SKATES —

The rubber-tired wheels of an old carpet sweeper can be used to advantage in making a pair of roller skates. In *Figure 1* is shown how an iron washer or two may be fastened to the wood with a piece of sheet metal to support the short axles of the wheels. The wheels are oiled through the holes *A* and *B, Figure 2*. These holes should be smaller than the axles. The two side pieces are fastened together with a board nailed on the top edges, as shown. This board also furnishes the flat top for the shoe sole.

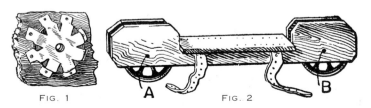

FIG. 1   A   FIG. 2   B

RUBBER-TIRED ROLLER SKATES.

Two straps are attached for fastening the skate to the shoe.

Pads will protect the knees of small children while using roller skates and will avoid many bruised knees and torn stockings. The pads are made by stitching several thicknesses of cloth together and sewing elastic to the upper and lower corners so the pads can be slipped over the legs.

— STURDY SWING HANGERS —

Made so there is no rubbing where it is fastened to the branch of a tree, this swing is sturdy enough for almost any child. The hangers are two lengths of flat iron that are bolted around the limb with pulleys attached to the hangers. The ropes are run through the sheaves and tied. There should be padding between the flat iron and the branch. Be sure to select a hearty branch that's up for the job.

— "FLYING-HORSE" SWING
HAS NOVEL DUAL CONTROLS —

Suspended from the porch ceiling, a sturdy tree limb or, in winter, from floor joists in the basement playroom, this tandem swing will provide hours of safe fun for the children. It has controls and foot treadles so arranged that each rider has to do his or her share of the work. A special feature of the construction is the three-point suspension, which helps to prevent the frame from tipping or swinging sidewise. Details show all the principal dimensions for a two-seated swing. Although any softwood can be used in the construction, the use of hardwoods, such as birch or oak, makes a more durable job that is easier to finish.

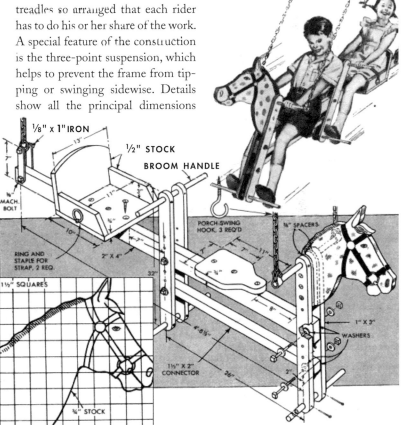

⅛" x 1" IRON

13"

½" STOCK

BROOM HANDLE

7"

⅜" MACH. BOLT

1"

RING AND STAPLE FOR STRAP, 2 REQ.

10"

2" X 4"

32"

1½" SQUARES

PORCH-SWING HOOK, 3 REQ'D

⅜" SPACERS

7"

11"

¾"

8"

4-8½"

1" X 3"

WASHERS

1½" X 2" CONNECTOR

26"

2"

¾" STOCK

— THRILLING RIDES IN THIS WAVE-ACTION SWING —

Suspended from vertical rocker arms, which in turn are cushioned with discarded auto-spring leaves, this novel swing gives the passenger a long, undulated slide. The stop blocks against which the springs operate can be spaced for the smoothest action. The wood need not even be surfaced, but below the ground it should be treated with creosote to prevent decay. The axis for the wig-wag supports consists of large machine bolts, with a section of brass tubing for a bearing.

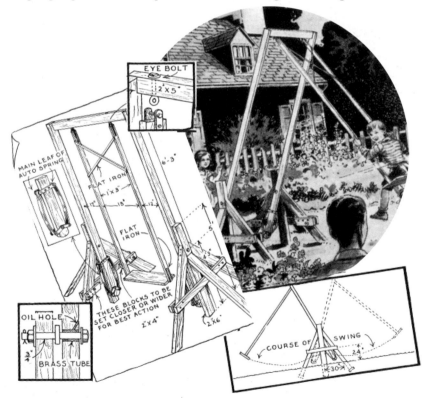

— DADDY BUILDS A BACKYARD SLIDE —

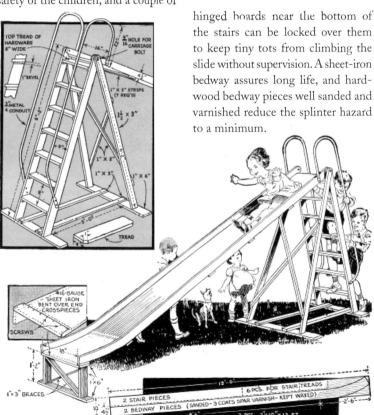

S et up in your backyard, this slide will afford your children and their friends many hours of pleasure safe from street traffic, and it can be dismantled and stored for the winter in a jiffy. A wide slide bedway, stairs, and "take-off plate" all make for safety of the children, and a couple of hinged boards near the bottom of the stairs can be locked over them to keep tiny tots from climbing the slide without supervision. A sheet-iron bedway assures long life, and hardwood bedway pieces well sanded and varnished reduce the splinter hazard to a minimum.

— A SAFE, QUICK CHANGE FROM SWING TO TRAPEZE —

What could be more fun than a swing that doubles as a trapeze? On swings that have chains instead of rope, it is possible to make the swing seat and a trapeze bar interchangeable by removing two links from each chain and inserting a repair link and heavy harness snap at the point the trapeze bar is to be attached. Eyebolts are fitted to the trapeze bar, the ends of the screws being peened so that the nuts can-not come off. The arrangement of fastening the chain to the seat with eyebolts, as shown, can be improved by providing yokes or hangers of an inverted V-shape at the ends of the seat to prevent tipping easily when children stand on it.

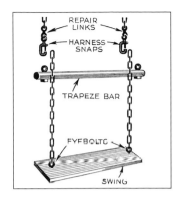

— TRAILER FOR A BICYCLE —

Instead of using a seat on the han-dlebars or frame of a bicycle for my little girl, I made a trailer, as shown in *Figure 1*, to attach to the rear axle. I made it from old bicycle parts. The handlebars, which form the back of the seat, fasten into the seat post of an old bicycle attached to the trailer axle. The trailer is attached to the rear axle of the bicycle with two arms

or forks, on the ends of which are two forgings, formerly used on the rear ends of a bicycle frame, brazed in, and each of the tube projections cut off from each to make a hook, as shown in *Figure 2*. The piece marked *E* shows one of these forgings or hooks in section. The original axle of the bicycle was removed and one 15/16 in. longer supplied, which was

FIG. 1—TRAILER ATTACHED TO A BICYCLE.

turned below the threads for clearance, as shown at *A*. A washer, *D*, with a hexagon hole was fitted over the regular nut *C*, on the axle, and filed, tapering so the forging or hook *E*, on the trailer attachment, could be kept in position. The washer *F* is held tightly against the hook by

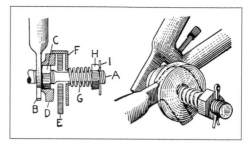

FIG. 2—THE HOOK IN POSITION.

pressure from a spring, *G*. The spring is held in place by a small nut, *H*, and cotter pin, *I*. This attachment makes a flexible joint for turning corners. When turning from right to left the left hook on the trailer fork stays in position, while the right hook pushes the washer *F* outward and relieves the strain on the fork. This attachment also makes it easy to remove the trailer from the bicycle. The washers *F* are pushed outward and the hook raised off the axle. —From a *Popular Mechanics* reader

CARNIVAL RIDES *and* OTHER BACKYARD THRILLS

— SPRINGBOARD —

To make this springboard, use a fairly flexible hardwood of suitable size. Note that the fixed end is hinged to a garage or other convenient building so that it can be folded up out of the way. Support for the board is provided by a post to which a crosspiece is nailed. Be sure that the post is driven solidly into the ground.

— PORTABLE SEESAW —

This seesaw consists merely of a plank balanced on an empty oil drum. To make it, cut two wooden blocks to fit the curvature of the drum and screw them to the plank. Bolt the plank and blocks to the drum, first cutting a hole in one end of the drum to allow tightening the bolts from the inside. A handhold can be made by driving a piece of broomstick into an undersize hole. The safer T-shape handhold may be made from pipe fittings, using a short nipple and tee for the vertical member. This is screwed into a pipe flange attached to the plank. Pipe nipples turned into the tee at the top of the pipe serve as handles.

— SKI-SKATES —

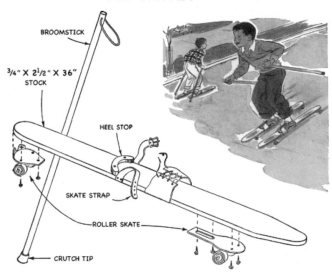

BROOMSTICK

¾" X 2½" X 36" STOCK

HEEL STOP

SKATE STRAP

ROLLER SKATE

CRUTCH TIP

"Ski-skates" provide much fun, and you don't need snow to ski. One pair of roller skates, in reasonably good condition, and two 3-ft. lengths of ¾-in. hardwood will make a pair of sidewalk skis. Cut off the "heel" of each roller-skate frame as indicated, shape the ends of the boards and smooth them with fine sandpaper, and then screw the two parts of each roller skate in place, as shown in the detail. Finish with leather ankle and toe straps and screw a curved heel stop to each ski. Suitable poles can be cut from discarded broom handles. Each is fitted with a wrist loop of strong cord and a crutch tip to prevent slipping.

— KIDDIE ROLLER COASTER —

Rollicking good times are ahead for the kids when Dad sets up this thrilling backyard roller coaster. The rider mounts the platform by steps at the rear and climbs aboard a four-wheel car. Depressing a trip lever starts the car on its way, sending it down the dips and up an inclined section of track. In climbing the incline, the car gradually loses speed and strikes a bumper at the end of the track. From there it rolls backward and finally comes to a stop at ground level. The car is returned to the starting platform by pushing it up the track. Having a platform only 3 ft. high and deep-flanged wheels which hold the car on the track, Rol-R-Ko is perfectly safe for three-year-old youngsters.

The toy is complete as originally built and pictured here, but if you have a large yard, the track can be extended to provide a much longer and more thrilling ride. This can be done by either adding additional dips down the line or merely letting the track run off on level ground, using flat, straight sections. The track sections are staked to the ground to assure a solid roadbed for the car. This, together with the flared structure which supports the elevated sections, eliminates any likelihood of the toy tipping over or the

28

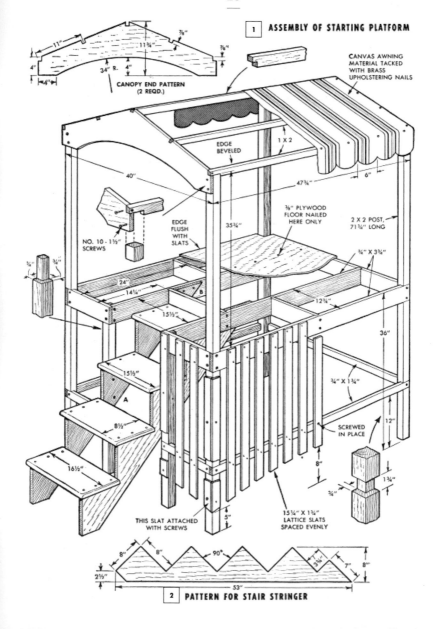

ASSEMBLY OF STARTING PLATFORM 1

11"

3/8"

11¾"

3/8"

4"

34" R.

4"

CANOPY END PATTERN (2 REQD.)

4"

CANVAS AWNING MATERIAL TACKED WITH BRASS UPHOLSTERING NAILS

EDGE BEVELED

1 X 2

40"

47¾"

6"

3/8" PLYWOOD FLOOR NAILED HERE ONLY

2 X 2 POST, 71¾" LONG

35¾"

EDGE FLUSH WITH SLATS

¾" X 3¾"

NO. 10 - 1½" SCREWS

¾" ¾"

24"

14¼"

B

12¾"

36"

15½"

15½"

A

¾" X 1¾"

8½"

16½"

SCREWED IN PLACE

12"

8"

1¾"

¾"

THIS SLAT ATTACHED WITH SCREWS

5"

15¼" X 1¾" LATTICE SLATS SPACED EVENLY

8"

8"

90°

3¾"

7"

8"

2½"

53"

PATTERN FOR STAIR STRINGER 2

track giving way under the weight of the rider. Rol-R-Ko is designed for easy dismantling in sections of a size convenient to handle and store. The canopy lifts off, both sides of the platform pull away and the steps slide out as a unit, leaving the floor and rear posts of the platform in one piece. The track itself is detachable from the platform by removing four screws, and, in turn, it comes apart in two sections.

The complete toy is constructed from common lumberyard material, No. 2 grade being good enough. The posts for the canopy are 2 x 2s, the platform framework is of 1 x 4s, the slats are common 1¾-in. lattice stock and the majority of the track and bracing is of 1 x 2s. The flanged cast-iron wheels for the car are standard items which can be purchased for ½-in. axles. Colorful awning material is selected for the canopy.

A simplified and less-expensive version of Rol-R-Ko is described on this page and shown in *Figure 5*. Here, the toy is stripped to the minimum, a straight length of track being substituted for the dipped section, which is merely extended off onto the ground with whatever number of straight sections of track you have room for. In either case, the basic construction of the platform is the same. The cutaway drawing in *Figure 1* details the assembly, with No. 10, 1½-in. screws being used throughout. Two 12-ft. lengths of 2 x 2s will make the four posts, with waste allowed for cutting. As shown in the lower detail of *Figure 1*, the posts are notched on two adjacent faces to receive the 1 x 4 platform framing and the 1 x 2 bracing at the bottom. Mortising the ends of the cross members of the framing in dado cuts makes for rigid construction, although plain butt joints can be used. The steps, *Figure 2*, are assembled as a separate unit and are fastened in place with eight screws at points *A* and *B* on both sides. A 4 x 4-ft. sheet of plywood is used to floor the platform. Note that this is notched at the corners to fit around the posts and is cut out for the steps. The plywood is nailed to the ends and all cross members of the platform, *but not along the sides,* as otherwise the sides of the structure cannot be removed. The slats around the sides of the platform are optional, although when painted alternately red and white they add considerably to the colorful carnival appearance of the toy. All of the slats are nailed in place except those that are indicated; namely, the end ones, *Figure 10*, those at each corner and the center one on each side. These must be attached

Lumber List
(Sizes are stock sizes—not actual)

1 pc. pine, 2 x 2 x 6 ft.—Stair posts
2 pcs. pine, 2 x 2 x 12 ft.—Corner posts
1 pc. pine, 1 x 10 x 10 ft.—Stair stringers
1 pc. pine, 1 x 10 x 6 ft.—Stair treads
1 pc. plywood, ¼ in. or ⅜ in. x 4 ft. sq.—Floor
1 pc. pine, 1 x 12 x 8 ft.—Canopy ends
5 pcs. pine, 1 x 2 x 4 ft.—Canopy stretchers
2 pcs. pine, 1 x 4 x 8 ft.— Platform framing
1 pc. pine, 1 x 4 x 10 ft.— Platform framing
1 pc. pine, 1 x 2 x 10 ft.— Platform stretchers
11 pcs. lattice, 1¾ x 10 ft.—Platform slats
1 pc. pine, 1 x 4 x 6 ft.—Platform track
2 pcs. pine, 1 x 8 x 10 ft.—Bandsawed rails
2 pcs. pine, 1 x 2 x 10 ft.—Straight rails
2 pcs. pine, 1 x 2 x 8 ft.—Track side rails
1 pc. pine, 1 x 2 x 12 ft.—Track crossties
8 pcs. lattice, 1¾ x 10 ft.—Track slats
1 pc. pine, 1 x 2 x 6 ft.—Braces (A)
1 pc. pine, 1 x 3 x 10 ft.—Brace legs Nos. 1
    and 6
1 pc. pine, 1 x 3 x 12 ft.—Rest of brace legs
1 pc. pine, 1 x 2 x 10 ft.—Brace cross cleats
1 pc. pine, 1 x 2 x 12 ft.—Track bracing
1 pc. pine, 1 x 4 x 3 ft.—Bumper
1 pc. pine, 1⅛ x 10 x 14 in.—For horse head
1 pc. pine, 1 x 13 x 26 in.—Base for car
1 pc. pine, 1 x 4 x 26 in.—Sides for car
1 pc. pine, 2 x 4 x 2 ft.—For bumper, etc.
(Waste from rails will make track coupling)

removed in dismantling the toy. Two screws at each corner of the canopy are used to fasten it to the upper ends of the posts. Each end of the canopy framework is cut from a 1 x 12-in. board and then notched along the top edges for joining both together with 1 x 2 stretchers. Unless you can buy 48- or 54-in. awning material, two separate pieces will have to be stitched together to cover the top. Eight scallops are cut along each edge and small copper nails are used to fasten the canopy in place.

The rails for the curved-track section, *Figure 3,* opposite, are bandsawed 2 in. wide from two 1 x 8 x 10-ft. pieces. Starting from the upper end, each board is marked off lengthwise according to the drawing and the various radii indicated are swung at these points, using a long flat stick for a compass. With help, both rails can be cut at one time and notched on the

with screws so that the slats can be taken off to get at the screws that are

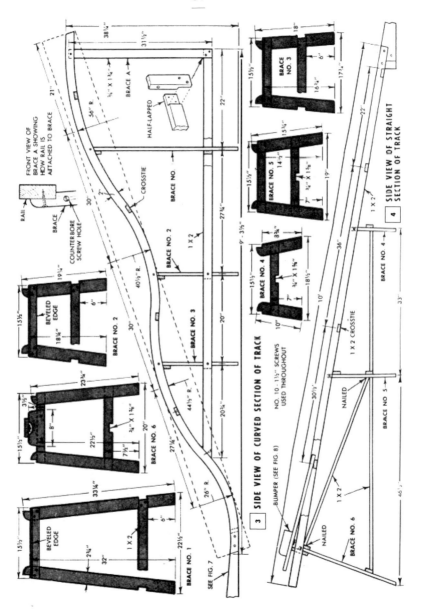

FRONT VIEW OF BRACE A SHOWING HOW RAIL IS ATTACHED TO BRACE

BRACE A

HALF-LAPPED

RAIL

BRACE

COUNTER BORE SCREW HOLE

CROSSTIE

BRACE NO. 2

BRACE NO. 3

BRACE NO. 1

BEVELED EDGE

BRACE NO. 2

BEVELED EDGE

BRACE NO. 6

SEE FIG. 7

SIDE VIEW OF CURVED SECTION OF TRACK

BRACE NO. 3

BRACE NO. 5

BRACE NO. 4

BUMPER (SEE FIG 8)

NO. 10 - 1½" SCREWS USED THROUGHOUT

SIDE VIEW OF STRAIGHT SECTION OF TRACK

BRACE NO. 4

1 X 2 CROSSTIE

NAILED

BRACE NO 5

1 X 2

NAILED

BRACE NO. 6

3
4

bottom edges for four crossties, 15½ in. long. A fifth crosstie at the lower end of the track is notched ½ in. deep at each end for wheel clearance and merely butted between the inner faces of the rails. The curved track is supported at the points indicated by braces, Nos. 1, 2 and 3. Brace No. 2 measures 19½ in. across the bottom. The legs of each one are cut from 1 x 3 stock and the crosspieces are 1 x 2s. Notches are cut on the outside of each leg for 1 x 2 side rails, 7 ft. 6½ in. long. The ends of these rails are half-lapped into braces A, which, in turn, are drilled and counterbored for screws that are used to attach the section to the platform.

The straight inclined section of track, *Figure 5,* is made similarly. Here, the rails are 10-ft. lengths of 1 x 2s, crosstied together as before and supported by brace Nos. 4, 5 and 6. Both sections of track are coupled together as shown in *Figure 8,* the outside pieces being notched to take the 1 x 2 ends of the inclined track. The coupling becomes a permanent part of the inclined section. The short section of track on the starting platform, *Figures 6* and *7,* is screwed to the plywood from the underside and is positioned to align with the abutting track. The manner in which the trip lever engages the rear axle of the car is shown in *Figure 6.* The lever should extend far enough behind the car to permit the rider to reach around and release it. The bumper, *Figure 9,* makes use of a screen-door spring to ease the shock when the front axle of the car strikes it. It's apparent from the drawing just how it works. The bumper itself is rabbeted along each side to fit a ⅞-in.

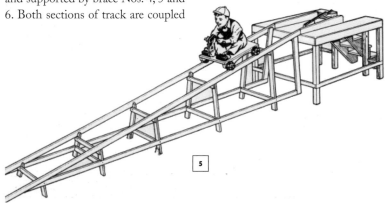

5

slot cut in a piece of 1 x 4. A nail driven through from one side of the slot engages the eye of the spring, while a screw and a large washer retain the bumper in the slot and yet allow it to slide freely. One end of the slotted member is fastened to a crosstie and the other end to a block screwed to brace No. 6, *Figure 3*. The top edges of the rails can be faced with a metal strip, if desired, although the wood will withstand considerable wear. Regular linoleum seam molding makes a neat facing.

The car is assembled as detailed in *Figure 11*. If you are unable to obtain a piece of wood 13 in. wide for the base of the car, it can be built-up by

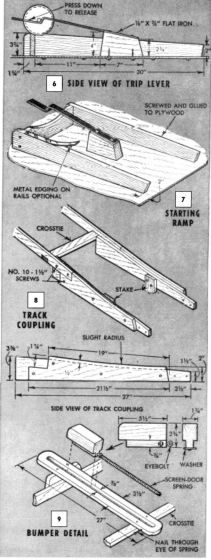

6 SIDE VIEW OF TRIP LEVER

7 STARTING RAMP

8 TRACK COUPLING

9 BUMPER DETAIL

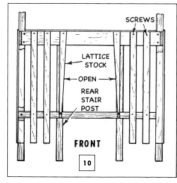

10 FRONT

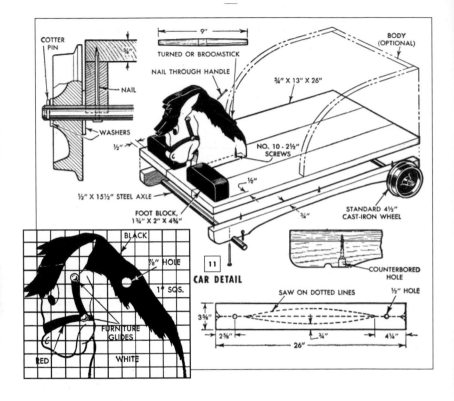

COTTER PIN

¾"

NAIL

WASHERS

½"

½" X 15½" STEEL AXLE

FOOT BLOCK,
1¾" X 2" X 4⅜"

9"

TURNED OR BROOMSTICK

NAIL THROUGH HANDLE

¾" X 13" X 26"

NO. 10 - 2½" SCREWS

½"

BODY (OPTIONAL)

STANDARD 4½" CAST-IRON WHEEL

¾"

BLACK

⅞" HOLE

1" SQS.

FURNITURE GLIDES

RED   WHITE

11

CAR DETAIL

COUNTERBORED HOLE

SAW ON DOTTED LINES

½" HOLE

3⅜"

2⅜"   ¾"   4¼"

26"

doweling and edge-gluing together several narrow pieces. Both side rails of the car are cut from a single piece of 1 x 4 in the manner shown in the detail below *Figure 11*. First, holes for the axles are drilled at each end and the piece is ripped in half through the center of the holes. Then each strip is bandsawed on the dotted lines. These pieces are screwed to the underside of the base flush with the side edges. Then, the axles for the wheels are placed in the half-round notches, drilled for an 8d nail and pinned as shown in the sectional detail, *Figure 11*. Drill a pilot hole for the nail so that it does not split the wood. A standard ½-in. washer placed on each axle between the wheel and the car will provide the correct tread. A paper pattern for the horse head is drawn full size from the squared outline given, then traced and cut from a piece of 1⅛-in.-thick wood. The head is drilled at the point indicated for a cross handle turned in a lathe or improvised from a broomstick. The handle is locked in position by driving a nail through it from the edge. The horse head is fastened securely to the base, 2 in. from the edge, with three long screws, and finally the foot blocks are screwed in place.

— HOMEMADE OVERHEAD TROLLEY COASTER —

The accompanying sketch shows a playground trolley line that furnished a great deal of amusement to many children at a minimum cost. The wire, which is 3/16 in. in diameter, was stretched between a tree and a barn across a vacant quarter block. The strength of the wire was first tested by a heavy man. When not in use the wire is unhooked from the tree and hauled into the barn and coiled loosely in the hay loft. The wire was made taut for use by a rope that was fastened to the beams in the barn. The trolley was made, as shown in *Figures 1* and *2,* of strips of

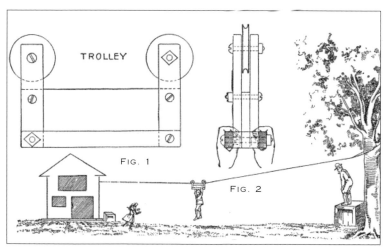

DETAILS OF THE TROLLEY AND HOW IT IS USED.

wood bolted with stove bolts on two grooved pulleys. The middle wide board was made of hardwood. The wheels were taken from light pulley blocks and stove bolts were purchased from a local hardware store to accurately fit the hubs. Because it was necessary to keep the bearings greased, we used Vaseline. This coaster made great sport for the youngsters and at no time were they in danger from a serious fall because the line was hung low and the slant of the wire was moderate.

— SEESAWS NEED NOT ALL BE ALIKE —

That's right. They needn't all be alike. They can have considerable variety. Here, for example, are four types, plus as many different kinds of fun.

Aerial The first one swings on a universal joint; that is, it can go up and down and around at the same time. One lass and a companion each grab an end. The lightweight really gets a ride 'round and 'round and up, too.

High-Lift Then there's this version. The upgoing passenger may feel as if she's about to take off from a springboard, but that's okay. If she hangs on to the sturdy handles provided she'll come down again. So will the other youngster when her turn comes. The detail drawing shows how it's made, in a sort of cantilever style. Posts should be anchored firmly in solid ground or concrete.

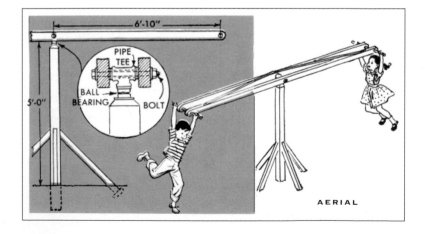

AERIAL

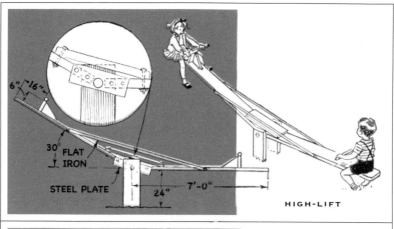

6" 16"

30° FLAT
IRON

STEEL PLATE   24"   7'-0"

HIGH-LIFT

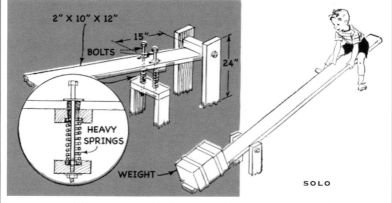

2" X 10" X 12"

15"

BOLTS

24"

HEAVY
SPRINGS

WEIGHT

SOLO

Solo These two are designed exclusively for solo flights. On one, as shown above, the dummy passenger is a box of sand. Find the right spot on the long end of the board where nice balance is attained and away you go. The other number, shown in the detail on the left, performs much like a springboard. Strong coil springs give the bounce necessary to keep things lively. Parts should be amply strong.

Lazy Louie This one's still different. Arms instead of legs supply the motive power. Riders about equally

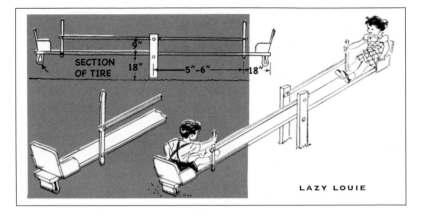

SECTION OF TIRE 9" 18" 5"–6" 18"

LAZY LOUIE

matched in weight sit in bucket seats and make with the hand levers. Sections cut from old tire casings and attached to the plank keep the bumps safe and satisfying. Operating this one by hand actually takes a lot more energy, but the riders never know the difference.

— OLD TRACTOR TIRES MAKES SANDBOX —

If you can lay your hands on a discarded tractor tire, you have the makings of a ready-made sandbox. And by driving a length of pipe in the center of it to hold an umbrella, you can protect young castle builders from the hot sun. Choose an umbrella you don't care about, since the handle must be cut off in order to stick the shaft into the pipe.

— PIRATE-SHIP SANDBOX WHEELS ABOUT THE YARD —

This ship sandbox will satisfy the desire of children to play "pirates" and to dig in the sand. Besides this, it's an unusual lawn ornament. The sail is a patchwork of old awning cloth, the shrouds and ratlines are awning cord, and the crow's nest is a coffee can. A forecastle serves as a locker for toys and a flag. The sail can be used as a sunshade, or it can be lowered to keep rain off the sand.

Pirate-ship SAND BOX wheels about the yard

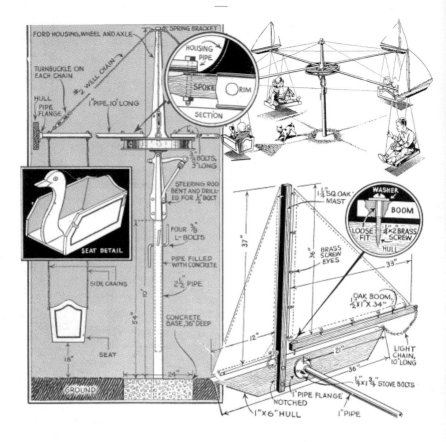

— SAILING MERRY-GO-ROUND —

Youngsters will get a thrill out of this wind-driven merry-go-round. Mounted on the front wheel and spindle of a car axle, it will rotate even in a breeze because of roller bearings in the wheel. One half of an axle housing is bolted to the wheel to hold chains for supporting the pipe arms, from which the seats are hung and to which dummy boats carrying the sails are attached. The assembly is supported by a pipe set 3 ft. in concrete. The stub end of the axle is inserted into the pipe and held by L-bolts.

— THIS LAWN "LAKE" KEEPS LITTLE TOTS IN BOUNDS —

Small children will be so interested in exploring the possibilities of this tiny "pond" that there'll be no time for experimenting with improvised playthings that might cause injury, or for wandering away as they so often do. The unit is built like a sandbox, except that the bottom and corner joints are taped and marine-glued. Waterproof plywood is best for the sides and bottom, although solid wood can be used for the sides. All exposed edges are rounded. Since children like bright colors, the box or tank may be painted lemon yellow with the seats in Chinese red and the sunshade column finished in the natural color of the wood.

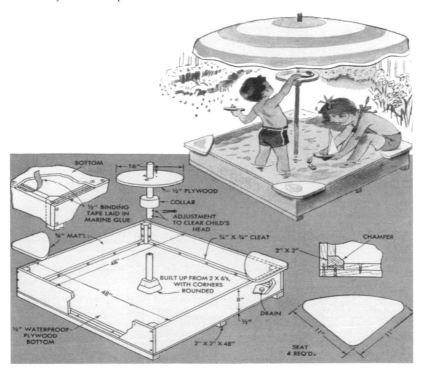

PLAYHOUSES *and* OTHER TEMPORARY RESIDENCES

— FAIRYLAND DOLLHOUSE FORMS PLAYHOUSE WHEN ENLARGED —

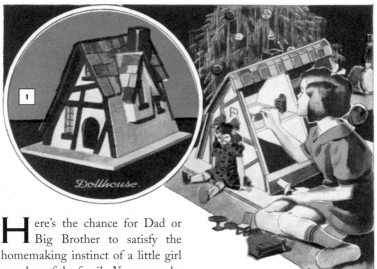

Dollhouse.

Here's the chance for Dad or Big Brother to satisfy the homemaking instinct of a little girl member of the family. You can make her either a small house in which to mother her dolls, or you can build the same house on an enlarged scale as an outdoor playhouse. *Figures 1* and *3* show the dollhouse, and *Figure 2,* the playhouse.

For the dollhouse, use ¼- or ⅜-in. plywood. Shape the sides, ends and roof pieces to size as in *Figure 4,* and cut the window openings. The inner edges are recessed to receive

the windows flush. Each one is cut out of two stiff pieces of cardboard. Tracing cloth is sandwiched between to simulate glass, *Figure 5.* Stain the cardboard walnut and set in the opening with glue. After the windows have been completed, paint the end and side pieces. Painting them now is much easier than after they have been fastened together. When dry, assemble them with brads, allowing the side sections to extend beyond the ends about ¼ in.

Now come the gables and chimney. It will be well to paint them too, before attaching the main section. The removable part of the roof is held in place by two cleats. The half-timbered effect is obtained by gluing or tacking on pieces of cardboard that have been stained and dried. Shingles are rectangular pieces of cardboard of various sizes glued or fastened with brads. They should be painted various colors such as orange, yellow, red, green or blue.

playhouse

FRONT   REAR

The house can be mounted on a piece of wood about ¾ in. thick or whatever size you want. When you are finished with the job, take a small watercolor brush and go over the outside with dark stain to produce a weathered appearance. The dollhouse can be illuminated with a string of Christmas-tree lights.

For those who would like to build a playhouse, *Figures 6* and *7* give detailed construction. The two sills which support the structure should rest either on stones or concrete blocks to prevent rot. For the floor joists use 2 x 4-in. stock and cover them with shiplap. The rafter sec-

tions are 1 x 3-in. stock, fastened together by overlapping boards.

Shakes are used for roofing, but if you are unable to obtain them, a good substitute can be made with ¼-in.-thick boards. As with the dollhouse, these should be varied in both width and length. Use either shiplap or waterproof plywood on the sides. Plywood is better as it will present a surface without cracks, and it can be laid out so that the joints are covered with the half timbers, which are used to produce the "fairyland" effect.

These timbers are 1 x 3-in. boards nailed over the wall as indicated. Paint the house as suggested for the dollhouse, or an all-white house with bright-colored shingles would be effective. The inside can be lined with wallboard, plywood, or even heavy cardboard, tinted or stained to suit. Or, you can use wallpaper. Linoleum and rugs for the floors will also please the young owner. Built-in furniture, such as a table, benches and bookcases, will make the house more "livable."

If desired, electrical lights can be installed with wall switches and ceiling lamps complete. Also, if you want the house as real as possible, you can put in running water, using small pipe or tubing to carry it where desired. If the house is placed permanently in the yard, a garden hose can be used to convey the water to the playhouse piping system.

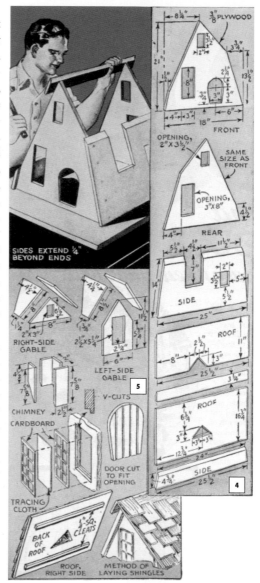

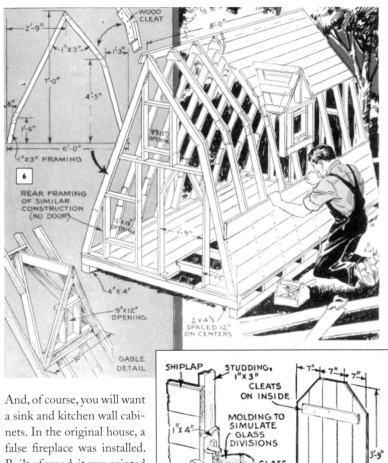

2'-9"

1"x3"

1"x3"

WOOD CLEAT

8'-0"

7'-0"

4'-5"

6"

1'-6"

6'-0"

1"x3" FRAMING

6

REAR FRAMING OF SIMILAR CONSTRUCTION (NO DOOR)

9"x12" OPENING

12"x12" OPENING

1'-9"

4"x4"

9"x12" OPENING

30"

GABLE DETAIL

2x4's SPACED 12" ON CENTERS

And, of course, you will want a sink and kitchen wall cabinets. In the original house, a false fireplace was installed. Built of wood, it was painted to simulate brick. The walls were insulated and an electrical heater installed. Also, there was a bell in the playhouse for calling the young mistress for meals.

SHIPLAP

STUDDING, 1"x3"

CLEATS ON INSIDE

7" **7"** **7"**

MOLDING TO SIMULATE GLASS DIVISIONS

1"x4"

GLASS

3'-9"

1"x2"

3/4"x1 1/2"

1/2"x1 1/4"

DETAIL OF WINDOW

7 **DOOR**

— BUILDING A HOUSE IN A TREE TOP —

LOFTY SENTRY BOX FOR GUARDING WATERMELON PATCH.

The accompanying photographs show a small house built in a treetop 20 ft. from the ground. The house is 5 ft. wide, 5 ft. 1 in. long, and 6 ft. 6 in. high. A small platform, 2 ft. wide, is built on the front. Three windows are provided, one for each side, and a door in front that opens onto the platform. But the entrance is made through a trap door in the floor of the house. This house was constructed by a youngster 14 years old and made for the purpose of watching over a melon patch.

— BUILD THIS KNOCK-DOWN PLAYHOUSE —

This trim little playhouse can be set up in 5 minutes and when taken down may be stored in a small space such as a closet. The walls are assembled as shown in the upper left-hand detail. A triangular corner piece to which part *B* is screwed, slides behind strips *C*, which are glued and nailed to the walls. The roof is supported by a ridge pole and held in place by pins projecting from the ends of the corner pieces. The chimney can be made of the same material as the walls. Two sides are notched to fit the roof angle and glued together. The door is held in place by a latch which is lifted through a finger hole in the door. Gaily colored flowers are painted on window boxes and shutters, which are shown in the crosshatched pattern.

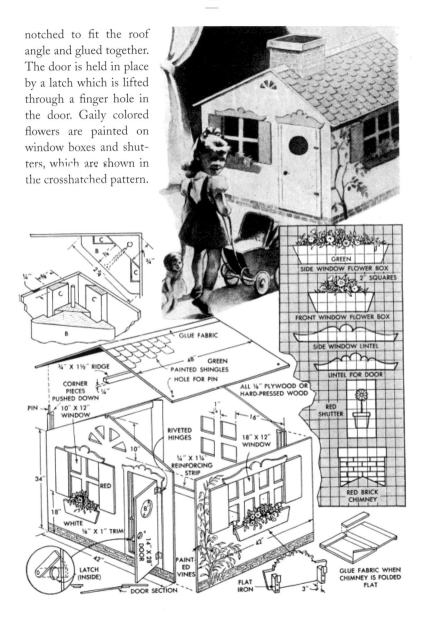

GREEN

SIDE WINDOW FLOWER BOX — 2" SQUARES

FRONT WINDOW FLOWER BOX

SIDE WINDOW LINTEL

LINTEL FOR DOOR

RED SHUTTER

RED BRICK CHIMNEY

GLUE FABRIC

¾" X 1½" RIDGE

48" GREEN PAINTED SHINGLES

HOLE FOR PIN

ALL ⅛" PLYWOOD OR HARD-PRESSED WOOD

CORNER PIECES PUSHED DOWN — ¼"

PIN — 10" X 12" WINDOW

RIVETED HINGES

18" X 12" WINDOW

¼" X 1¼" REINFORCING STRIP

34"

10"

RED

18"

WHITE

⅛" X 1" TRIM

14" X 28" DOOR

42"

LATCH (INSIDE)

DOOR SECTION

PAINTED VINES

42"

FLAT IRON

3"

GLUE FABRIC WHEN CHIMNEY IS FOLDED FLAT

Go Fly *a* Kite

— Kites of Many Kinds and How to Make Them —

One of the prettiest of all is the butterfly kite. To make this get two thin kite sticks of equal length. Bend each in an arc, tying one end of a strong string to one end of each stick and the other end of the string to a point about 3 in. from the other end of the stick. This leaves one end of each stick free, hooking over the hemisphere described by the thread and the stick. Now tie another thread to each of these free ends and tie the other end of the thread to a point near the other end of the stick, corresponding with the distance

BUTTERFLY KITE

from the end at which the first strings were tied on the opposite side. This done, you should have two arched frames, each an exact counterpart of the other in size, curvature and weight. Now fasten the two frames together so that the arcs will overlap each other, as shown in the sketch. Bind the intersecting points securely with thread.

To make the butterfly's head, secure two heavy broom straws or two short wires, and attach them to the top part of the wing frames near where the sticks intersect, so that the straws or wires will cross. These form the antennae, or the "smellers." Then select the color of paper you want: yellow, brown, blue, white or any other color. Lay it on a flat surface and

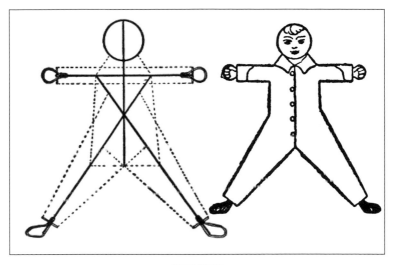

BOY KITE

place the frame on top of it, holding the frame down securely with a weight. Then with a pair of scissors cut the paper around the frame, leaving about a ½-in. margin for pasting. Cut slits in the paper about 2 in. apart around the curves and at all angles to keep the paper from wrinkling when it is pasted. Distribute the paste with a small brush and make the overlaps a little more than ¼ in. wide and press them together with a soft cloth. When the kite is dry decorate it with paint or strips of colored paper in any design you may fancy. The best effects are produced by pasting pieces of colored paper on top of the other

paper. Black paper decorations show up to fine advantage when the kite is in flight. Attach the "belly-band" to the curved sticks by punching a hole in the same manner as it is attached to the common hexagonal or coffin-shaped kites. With a tail, your kite is ready to fly.

Another interesting design is the boy kite, which always attracts attention and affords splendid sport for the American youth in springtime. In making a boy kite it should be remembered that the larger the boy is, the better he will fly. To construct the frame, two straight sticks, say, 3½ ft. long, should serve for the legs and body; another straight stick forms the spine and should be about 2 ft. 4 in. long. For the arms, get a fourth straight stick about 3 ft. 3 in. long. Make the frame for the head by bending a light but tough stick in a circle about 7 in. in diameter. Bind it tightly with a strong thread and through its center run the spine. Then tack on the arm stick 3 in. under the circle so that the spinal column crosses the arm stick exactly in the center. Wrap tightly with strong thread and tack on the two sticks that are to serve for the legs and body. The leg sticks should be fastened to the arm stick about 6 in. on either side of the spinal column, and crossed so that the other ends are 3 ft. apart. Tack them and the arm stick together at the point where they intersect. Small hoops and cross stick of the same material as the head frame should be fastened to both extremities of the arm stick and the lower ends of the leg sticks for the hands and feet. See that both hand frames are exactly alike and exercise equal caution regarding the foot frames; also see that the arm stick is at exact right angles with the spine stick and that the kite joints are all firmly tied and the kite evenly balanced; otherwise it may be lopsided. Fasten on the strings of the frame, beginning at the neck at equal distances from the spine, as indicated by the dotted lines in the diagram. Extend a string slantingly from the arm stick to the head on both sides of the spinal column, and run all the other strings as shown in the cut, being careful that both sides of the frame correspond in measurements.

To cover the kite, select different colors of paper to suit your taste, and after pasting them together, lay the paper on the floor and, placing the frame on it, cut out the pattern. Leave an edge of ½ in. all around and make a slit in this edge every 6 in. and at each angle; make the slits 2 in. apart around the head. After the kite is pasted and dry, paint the buttons, hair, eyes, hands, feet, etc., as you desire. Arrange the "bellyband" and tail band and attach the kite string in the same manner as in the ordinary coffin-shaped kite.

The "lady kite" is made on the same principle as the boy kite. The frame is made exactly as the boy kite and then "dressed" with tissue paper to represent a girl. Remember the dotted lines represent the strings or thread, and the other lines indicate kite sticks. Be careful with your measurements so that each side of the kite corresponds exactly and is well balanced. Also see that every point

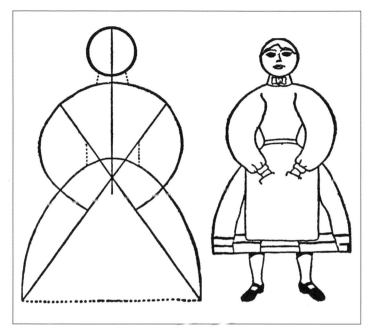

GIRL KITE

where the sticks intersect is firmly tacked and bound.

To cover the kite, first paste together pieces of tissue paper of different colors to suit your taste. The paste should be made of flour and water and boiled. Make the seams or overlaps not quite ⅜ in. wide. Lay the paper on the floor, using weights to hold it down, and place the frame of the kite upon it. Then cut out the paper around the frame, leaving an edge of ½ in. Don't forget to make a slit in the edge every 6 or 7 in. and at each angle. Around the head the slits are cut 2 in. apart, as in the case of the boy kite. After the kite is dry, paint the paper however your fancy dictates.

To make the breast band, punch holes through the paper, one upon each side of the leg sticks, just above the bottom, and one upon each side of the arm sticks at the shoulders. Run one end of the string through the hole at the bottom of the left limb and tie it to the leg stick; tie the other end at the right shoulder. Fasten one end of another string of the same length at the bottom of the right leg; pass the string up across the first band and tie the other end at the left shoulder. Attach the kite string to the breast band at the point where the two strings intersect. Tie the knot so that you can slide the kite string up or down until it is properly adjusted. The tail band is made by tying a string to the leg sticks at the bottom of the breast band. Let the string hang slack below the skirt and attach the tail to the center. The same general rules apply in attaching the string and tail to the boy kite.

You can make the lady look as if dancing and kicking in the clouds by making the feet of stiff pasteboard and allowing them to hang loose from the line which forms the bottom of the skirt. The feet will move and sway with each motion of the kite.

— HOMEMADE KITE REEL —

This kite reel is constructed from two old pulleys and a few pipe fittings. The large pulley is about 14 in. in diameter, on the face of which are riveted flat strips of iron with extending arms. These arms are reinforced by riveting smaller pieces from one to the other. If you like high-flying kites this is an efficient way to handle your kite line.

OLD PULLEYS AND PIPE FITTINGS.

— THE W-KITE —

The W-Kite, one of the highest fliers and most efficient climbers of all kites, combines the stability of the regular box kite and the strength of the triangular box kite. It flies well without a tail and, in a fair breeze, will "walk" right up to a spot almost directly overhead. It does not pull hard, as does the box, because it adjusts itself constantly. In a fair breeze, it can be fed into the air from the hand and brought back to the hand without ever touching the ground.

The frame is made of any light wood and covered with cellophane. The joints of the frame are tied with string or heavy thread and then coated with shellac or glue. The cellophane cover should not be pulled too tightly, as it may shrink. Where necessary, back the cellophane with a light network of thread tied to the frame. A four-legged bridle is used, the length of the top two legs being about the same as the kite's short struts. The method of attaching the bridle can be seen in the illustration. The size of the kite may be varied, provided the proportions of the parts remain the same as pictured.

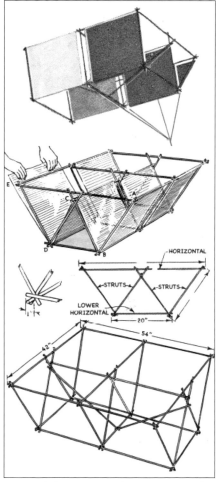

— DROPPING PARACHUTES ADDS ZEST TO KITE FLYING —

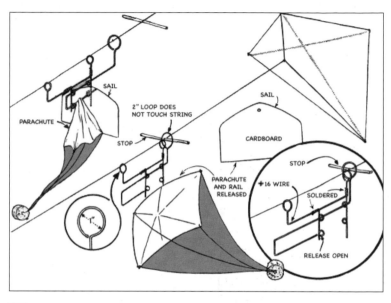

SAIL

PARACHUTE

2" LOOP DOES NOT TOUCH STRING

STOP

SAIL

CARDBOARD

PARACHUTE AND RAIL RELEASED

STOP

#16 WIRE

SOLDERED

RELEASE OPEN

Parachutes carried up to a lofty kite, and automatically released when the carrier hits a cross stick tied in the kite line, will keep up a lively interest. The carrier must be lightweight and there should be very little friction on the line so that ascent of the carrier will not be impeded. A cardboard sail and a parachute are held on a sliding member, which is pushed back when it strikes the cross stick, releasing sail and parachute. By going over the details you will see how the device works.

— NOVEL HOLDER FOR KITE STRING —

A wooden cleat riveted to a belt to go around your waist provides a novel holder for kite string. The string is wound on the cleat and unwound as desired. If the end is tied to the cleat, there will be no danger of the kite getting away. Sometimes the simplest ideas are also the best ones.

{ CHAPTER 2 }

GARDENING PROJECTS *for* GREEN THUMBS

THE TOOLS *to* MAKE YOUR GARDEN GROW

— PINT-SIZED RAKE FOR SHRUBS —

Cutting down a bamboo rake to five to six teeth made the handiest tool I ever had for raking between shrubs. I cut away the outer teeth and retwisted wire lacing to hold remaining teeth intact, as shown in the detail above.

—From a *Popular Mechanics* reader

— CONVERT TABLE FORK TO RAKE —

When you're in need of a small garden cultivator to loosen the surface around plants, you can make one simply by converting an old table fork to this use. The tines should be bent at right angles to the handle, as illustrated. The cultivator is small enough to carry in a garden-tool caddy.

— NAIL KEG MADE TO SERVE AS STORAGE "KIT" FOR SMALL GARDEN TOOLS —

Small garden tools are less likely to be mislaid if they are kept in this portable kit. It is nothing more than a small nail keg fitted with a hinged lid of plywood and a carrying handle. To attach the lid, a wooden block is bandsawed to the contour of the keg and screwed flush with the top to take the hinges. A hook and screw eye keep the lid closed when the kit is being carried. The carrying handle is attached to the center of the top side of the lid. As shown in the illustration, a wooden bracket and cup hooks will provide a means of holding the tools.

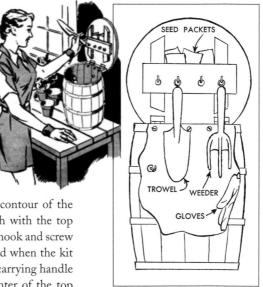

SEED PACKETS

TROWEL WEEDER

GLOVES

— SERVICEABLE GARDEN RAKE MADE FROM UMBRELLA RIBS —

A serviceable garden rake strong enough to gather fallen leaves and rake grass clippings, yet flexible enough not to injure tender growing plants if accidentally pulled across them, can be made from a few umbrella ribs. They are flattened at one end and held in place by being clamped tightly between two pieces of ¼-in. plywood or hard-pressed board bolted together as shown. A handle can be made from a length of broomstick notched at the lower end to fit over the plywood.

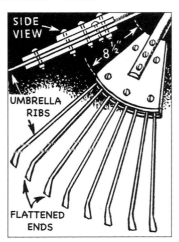

— MAKE A SMALL WEEDER —

Make this handy garden weeder from an old paintbrush handle, discarded hacksaw blade and four screws. It's the perfect tool for working in small gardens between narrowly spaced rows, and will rescue your hands from chafing.

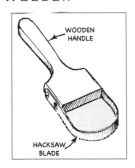

— LEAKY HOSE MAKES HANDY GARDEN SPRINKLER —

Don't throw away that leaky old garden hose. A section of it will still make itself useful if you punch holes through it along one side and plug the open end. You'll then have a handy garden sprinkler.

— UMBRELLA BASKET —

Here's how one small commercial grower of choice "glads" solved the problem of handling and transporting the fragile blooms from the row to the packing bench. He cut and fitted a cardboard cone over the brace ribs of an old umbrella, as indicated by the dotted lines in the detail. The cone forms the bottom of the basket. The umbrella is then placed alongside the row in inverted position and the blooms are laid with the stems all in one direction around the full circumference of the "basket." In this way the delicate blooms are not crushed or the stems bent by being stacked. When filled, the basket is easily carried.

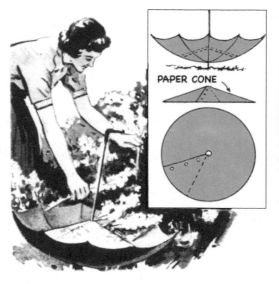

PAPER CONE

— REPAIRING LEAK IN GARDEN HOSE —

You can patch a leak in a garden hose with a cold patch of the type used on inner tubes if you have a clamp like the one shown to put pressure on the patch while the cement is setting. If the hose has a corrugated or ribbed surface, it will have to be smoothed down.

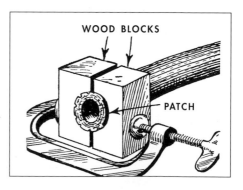

WOOD BLOCKS

PATCH

— SOAKER HOSE STORES NEATLY ON A WOODEN REEL —

Rolling up a soaker hose can be a bothersome chore, but not anymore. With this crank-type holder, you can reel it in and pay it out as easily as you would a kite string. The detail shows how simple it is to make. You can save yourself the job of threading the ground spike by buying a length of ready threaded rod at your hardware store. Two jam nuts provide a shoulder on the rod for the hardwood arms. Make the holes in the arms slightly oversize to assure free reeling. The reel knob is a piece of dowel drilled through the center for a wood screw.

— FORESTALL BENDING OF HOSE —

A plastic hose support at the coupling joined to the hose bib will forestall bending, which tends to reduce water pressure. A short length of BX cable from which the wires have been removed can provide helpful reinforcement.

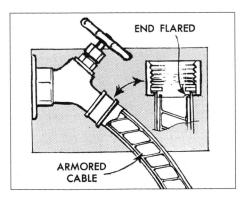

END FLARED

ARMORED CABLE

— PICKET-LEG TOTE BOX —

At berry-picking time, strawberry plants may be ruined and berries crushed if a full tote box is set down on them. To avoid this, the box shown below has pointed legs like fence pickets; they will not crush plants.

— STRAIGHTEN A TREE —

There are many reasons why a tree trunk leans to one side or the other. Why not try a tree straightener, which will often do the job in a single growing season? It consists of a notched stick, some twine and a brick. Hang the brick as shown, opposite the bends, to exert a constant pull that should eventually correct the problem. Off-the-ground bracing is a help when mowing.

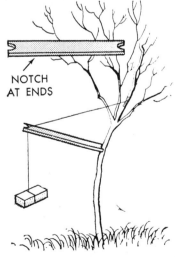

NOTCH AT ENDS

— AN EFFECTIVE CHERRY PICKER —

An effective implement can be easily made for picking cherries rapidly with a minimum of climbing. A frame is made of stiff wire or light iron rod, the ends being brought together and forced tightly into a handle of the proper length. On the front of the frame a series of picking fingers or hooks is fastened, about ¼ in. apart, so that the fruit cannot pass between them. *Figures 1* and *2* illustrate two methods of attaching the hooks. Solder should be used in both cases to make the fingers rigid. The device is completed by attaching a bag of close-woven fish netting to catch the fruit as it is plucked from the tree.

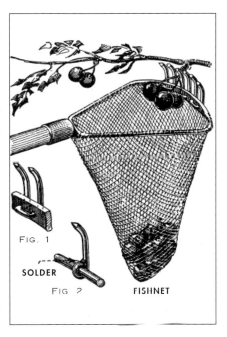

FIG. 1

SOLDER

FIG. 2   FISHNET

IT ALL STARTS *with a* SEED

— TEST LAST YEAR'S SEEDS —

To test germination of seeds left over from last year, sprinkle a few on a dampened cotton cloth and roll it up. Store in a warm place for several days and keep damp. If seeds sprout, you can plant them.

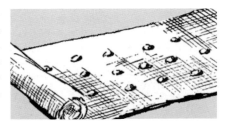

— Start Seedlings —

Half-gallon milk cartons make waterproof planting flats for starting seedlings when cut in half and filled with a planting mix. Sow seeds in a well-tamped mix, then place the flats next to a window offering sunlight. Cover flats with a pane of glass to keep temperature and moisture constant.

— Plant Rows in Line —

Although plants are said to grow just as well in a crooked row, such a planting can have little eye appeal for the serious gardener even though her plants may thrive ever so luxuriously. Straight, uniformly spaced rows are easy to achieve at planting time if you use a cord and stake that will hold the cord taut. Pointed wooden stakes will do, of course, but it takes only a little more time to make better, longer-lasting stakes by bending 30-in. lengths of 5/16-in. steel rod to the shape indicated. The loop formed at the center of the rod is made large enough to take the toe of your shoe, enabling you to drive the stake into

the ground just as you would a spade. A handle, bent at the upper end of the stake, allows you to stretch the cord taut simply by inclining the stake slightly as it is driven.

— GARDEN ROW MARKERS —

Durable row markers for the garden can be made from short lengths of water pipe and spring-type clothespins. Drive the pipe into the ground and insert one leg of the clothespin in the end of the pipe. Then catch an empty seed package in the jaws of the clothespin to mark the crop. Or fasten the clothespin to the top of a wooden stake with a nail.

— BEANS SERVE AS MARKERS IN ROWS OF SLOW-GROWING SEEDS —

Because the slow growth of carrot seed often left him in doubt as to where he could cultivate safely before the plants showed above the ground, one gardener planted a few string beans in the same trenches. These seeds grow rapidly, and when one or two of them are planted about a foot apart all along each row, the appearance of these plants in a few days serves as a marker.

BEAN PLANTS

— SEEDLING SUNSHADES —

Protect seedlings from the sun during the first few critical days after transplanting by propping berry boxes over them. Light and ventilation are ample for plant growth.

— Seedling Transplanter —

Moving tiny seedlings from flats to a cold frame of the open row may result in a considerable loss unless you have the proper tool. Make one from an 8-in. length of 1-in.-diameter aluminum tubing. Just saw into the tube on an easy curve to the center, then along the axis about 3 in. and end with a curved cut similar to the first one. This gives you a narrow trowel point, as shown,

just right for lifting seedlings—roots, soil and all—from the flat.

— Protection from Frost —

Plastic covers used for protecting transplants from late frost should be supported with several wire arches to keep from crushing them. Supports are formed from short lengths of clothes-hanger wire.

— Avoid Soil Drain —

Keep soil from washing away when watering newly planted shrubs by slitting a heavy aluminum-foil pie tin radially and then centering it on the shrub trunk as shown at right. Holes in the bottom of the pie tin let water drain slowly.

— PICNIC FORKS PIN PLANT BRANCHES TO GROUND TO START NEW GROWTH —

When you want to hold a branch or trailer of certain kinds of plants close to the ground so that they will take root at the joints and start new growths, try using wooden picnic forks for the purpose. Just slip the fork over the branch as shown and press it into the ground, taking care not to force the fork deep enough to pinch and damage the tender plant. Once the plants take root or yield new growths at the joints, you can remove the forks.

PICNIC FORK

— GOOD STAKE TO SUPPORT PLANTS —

Tall-growing plants, such as tomatoes, dahlias, giant zinnias and others need to be supported by staking before they reach ultimate growth. One simple way of doing this is by means of a wooden stake, which is driven into the ground near the plant, and a loop of heavy wire passed around the plant 18 or 20 in. above the ground, the free ends of the wire being forced through small holes drilled near the top of the stake. If possible, the stake should be driven at the same time the plants are set

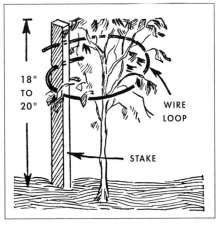

18" TO 20"

WIRE LOOP

STAKE

out in the garden to avoid damage to the roots.

— SOAK A FLOWER BED —

A safe way to soak a flower bed without the risk of washing away plants is to attach an old cotton work glove over the end of a hose with twine or a rubber band. This breaks the stream of water and protects plants.

— TRANSPLANTING WITH EASE —

To accomplish transplanting without disturbing the delicate plant root system, line the starting container with a plastic bag. Don't forget to punch a few drainage holes in the bottom of the bag.

PLASTIC BAG

— PORTABLE GARDEN FRAME —

Protect young plants with a portable garden frame made from a pair of modified coat hangers and two panes of glass. A batten with holes drilled through it slips over the hangers to brace them and hold the glass.

— REPAIR A BROKEN STEM —

Next time you break the stem of a favorite plant, bind the sections together with cellulose tape. If done in time, the break will heal, restoring the plant to its original healthy condition.

— EASY INSECTICIDE APPLICATION —

Trying to dust plants with insecticide on a windy day can be a hopeless task. It can even be dangerous as the insecticide can end up on your skin or even in your eyes instead of on your plants. However, if you drop an old lamp shade over each plant before dusting, as shown, you'll have a perfect windbreak for confining the spray.

TRELLISES, ARBORS *and* OTHER THINGS BOTH PRETTY *and* PRACTICAL

— BEAUTIFYING YOUR HOME GARDEN —

The homeowner who is able to use a few carpenters' tools can, at slight expense, add considerably to the appearance and value of her house. Few city or suburban lots are so small that there is no room for a simple rose arbor or trellis, a screen to hide an ugly alley view or to improve the appearance of the unattractive though useful garage, or a small pergola, even if it has no Corinthian columns leading to a long vista of formal garden. The examples shown in the accompanying illustrations are mostly very simple, and as before stated, need but little skill beyond the ability to handle hammer and saw, and occasionally a turning or keyhole saw.

The first thing is the selection of the lumber. The best all-around material for garden furniture of this type is cypress, or, if this is unobtainable locally, good yellow pine. It is sometimes hard to get cypress in "dimension" sizes, such as 4 x 4-in., and then yellow pine, which is generally available, can be used. Fir is also a good weathering wood, and one that takes paint well. Where round posts are needed for any purpose, these will usually be of cedar, which is likewise a suitable wood. Lattice is mostly of cypress and comes in standard 1-, 1¼-, 1½-, 2- and 2½-in. widths.

Remember when ordering your lumber that this always comes in even lengths, beginning at 10 ft., then 12, 14, 16, 18 ft. and so on, so that if you order an 8-ft. board, it will have to be cut from a longer one and you will pay for the cutting and for the waste material. It pays to figure a little before ordering the lumber for any job, to see that the stock will cut without waste, or that the project can be built from standard sizes. Also, remember that lumber sizes are always the size of the rough lumber, before planing, so that a two-by-four is really not more than 1¾ x 3¾ in.

All posts that are to be sunk in the ground, like the bearing posts of arbors, fences, and pergolas, should either have their butts painted with liquid tar before being placed in position, or at least be thoroughly painted with two or three coats of paint. A thorough soaking with creosote is also good to minimize rotting. Also, these posts should be sunk at least 3 ft. in the ground, or below the frost level, so that the heaving of the ground will not throw the whole structure out of plumb the first winter.

Another important thing is the fastenings of the structures. Use galvanized roofing nails or brass screws, which will not rust. Fastenings that rust not only mark the paint, but also allow the structure to fall apart after it has been up a year or two. When making joints in the woodwork, slap a paintbrush full of paint on the joint before fastening the pieces together to prevent unwelcome moisture from creeping in and helping to rot the joints.

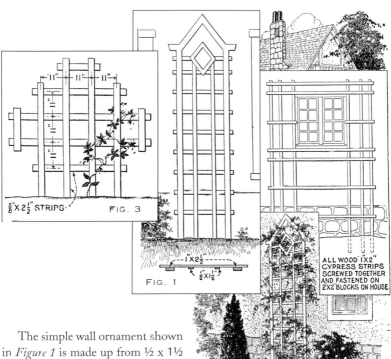

FIG. 3

$\frac{5}{8}"X 2\frac{1}{2}"$ STRIPS

FIG. 1

$1"X2\frac{1}{2}"$

$\frac{1}{2}"X1\frac{1}{2}"$

FIG. 2

ALL WOOD 1X2"
CYPRESS STRIPS
SCREWED TOGETHER
AND FASTENED ON
2X2 BLOCKS ON HOUSE

The simple wall ornament shown in *Figure 1* is made up from ½ x 1½ and 1 x 2½-in. cypress. The whole thing is assembled on the ground or in the home shop before erection, and then fastened to the wall with galvanized nails or brass screws, set into wood plugs, driven tightly into holes in the wall, if of brick. If the house is of frame construction, the wooden plugs are, of course, unnecessary, but 2 x 2-in. blocks should first be nailed to the wall, and the ornament fastened to the blocks. The important thing to observe in this, as in all latticework, is to space the cross or lattice strips evenly. Unevenly spaced latticework is apparent at once, and completely spoils the appearance of the finished work.

Another very simple trellis for the bottom of a low wall, or on which to train a small climber, is shown in *Figure 2*. The strips here are ⅝ x

2½ in., spaced 11 in. on centers each way. Still another, spanning a window, is shown in *Figure 3,* and here the vertical strips should be carried down below the frost line, if they are allowed to go into the ground at all. However, they may be cut off about ¼ in. above the ground if desired, well fastened to the wall, on 2 x 2-in. blocks, as specified.

An attractive design for an interior corner of a wall is shown in *Figure 4,* and can be used either as a corner seat or as a stand for a flowerpot. Used either way, it makes a charming decoration. Full details are given in the illustration opposite.

In *Figure 5* is shown an arch for the window, and here the amateur is likely to run up against her first

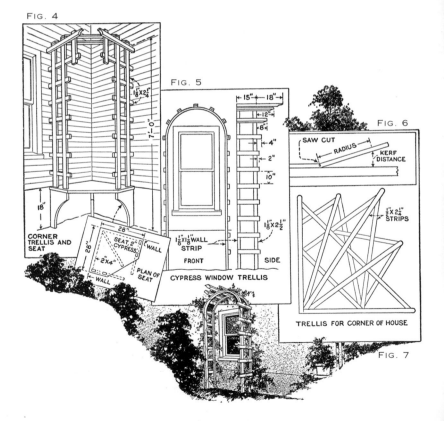

FIG. 4

FIG. 5

FIG. 6

FIG. 7

CORNER TRELLIS AND SEAT

CYPRESS WINDOW TRELLIS

TRELLIS FOR CORNER OF HOUSE

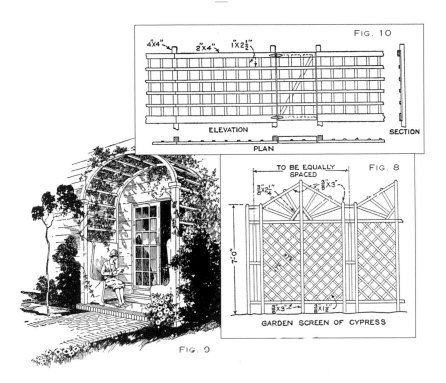

FIG. 10

4"X4" 2"X4" 1"X2½"

ELEVATION   SECTION

PLAN

TO BE EQUALLY SPACED   FIG. 8

3"X2¼"   3"X3"

7'-0"

GARDEN SCREEN OF CYPRESS

FIG. 9

hard job, in bending the arch strips. The strips can be bent, however, by steaming them for half an hour or so, or by soaking them where the bend is to be made, for the same time in hot water. Steaming is best. Failing the necessary apparatus for this, the strips can be bent by cutting, as detailed in *Figure 6*. First make a saw kerf in the piece, at the place where the arch springs, about as deep as it is thought the kerfs should be.

Measure from this point a distance equal to the radius of the arch and make a mark on the strip. Now lay the strip down on the bench top or on a level place on the sidewalk, and raise the end of the strip until the edges of the saw kerf meet. The distance from the radius mark on the strip to the bench top or sidewalk will be the proper distance apart to make the saw kerfs. It will probably be found that cutting the kerfs half the thickness of the strip will be about right, but they must all be of uniform depth. The same method can be used for many other garden arches.

A trellis for the corner of the house is shown in *Figure 7*. The strips here again are ½ x 2½ in., fastened to the house as were the others.

To screen off an undesirable view, or to divide the flower garden from the vegetable garden, the attractive screen shown in *Figure 8* may be used. No overall dimensions are given for this, as these depend on the location. The spacing of the main members of the screen may be altered to suit the space at hand. This design may be modified in many ways; for instance, the triangular top work of the panels may be omitted, and the plain latticework instead carried up to within a couple of inches of the top of the vertical columns. The vertical members are ⅜ x 3 in., on each side of the latticework, and they should be sunk in the ground at least 4 ft.

On all work of this kind, where the sections are of considerable size, the best job is done by setting the posts or vertical members in concrete. If this is undesirable, the soil must be packed solidly around them, and the structure should be temporarily braced to posts on the side until the fill has packed down hard

and will support the structure solidly. This is especially necessary in the case of screens, as they, unlike arbors and trellis arbors, have no side support.

Leaving the backyard for the moment, *Figure 9* shows how the arch trellis can be applied to the front of the house. The benches can be made of pine or fir, and the whole makes a very attractive entrance for the cottage or the colonial type of small house.

Three simple and attractive fences of the garden are shown in *Figures 10* through *12*. Here the important things to remember are to keep the posts exactly in line, and to place them such a distance apart that the stock selected will cut without waste and still come evenly on the centers of the posts. The best way to erect the fence is to set up the end posts first, plumbing them until they are exactly perpendicular, and then stretch a line between them. Set the intermediate posts to line and plumb them, and the fence will be right. This applies to posts for pergolas and long arbors also.

Figure 13 shows a very attractive combination garden entrance and seat, but the same design, without the seat or gate, can be used in any part of the garden. The design can also be adapted for use as a pergola. We have not shown any pergolas

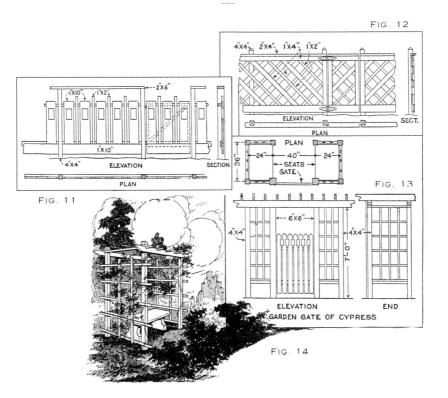

FIG. 12

FIG. 11

FIG. 13

FIG. 14

ELEVATION
GARDEN GATE OF CYPRESS

using round columns, as these are rather expensive, and, in any event, if the reader wants a pergola of this type, she can easily get a design from the catalogs of houses supplying this material.

So much of this work depends on individual taste that only a few of the designs shown are fully dimensioned. The other sketches accompanying this article contain suggestions that will enable the owner to work out her own sizes and details. In general, the amateur will be advised to stick to designs employing straight lines, and to avoid curves as much as possible. The ends of rafters or pergolas and arbors, etc. can be ornamented in several very simple ways, as illustrated in various drawings, with no more tools than a compass or keyhole saw and a brace and expansion bit.

— SETTING TRELLIS WORK —

There is no question about the improvement that can be effected in the looks of the home by the employment of simple trellises, but the common method of setting these has one great defect. In this method the bottom of the trellis is nailed to a post sunk in the ground,

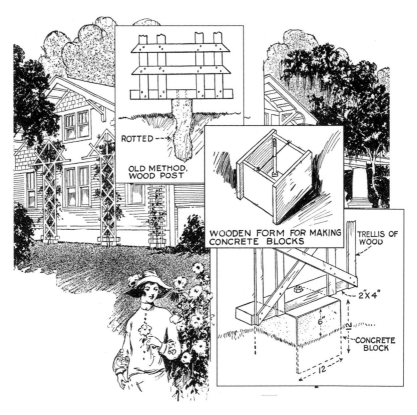

ROTTED

OLD METHOD, WOOD POST

WOODEN FORM FOR MAKING CONCRETE BLOCKS

TRELLIS OF WOOD

2"X4"

6"

CONCRETE BLOCK

12

A MUCH BETTER METHOD OF SETTING TRELLIS WORK THAN THE ORDINARY ONE OF USING WOODEN POSTS IS THIS, IN WHICH CONCRETE BLOCKS FORM A PERMANENT SETTING, AND ONE THAT WILL NOT ROT OR DECAY.

and this rots in time. A much better way to set the trellises permanently is shown in the illustration. A simple wooden form is made that will hold 1 cu. ft. of concrete, as shown in the detail, and a bolt, about ½ x 14 in., is suspended by means of a twisted wire so that the head of the bolt is about 2 in. from the bottom of the form. The wire can be fastened to two nails partly driven into the upper edges of the box at the center. The form is then filled with concrete. After the concrete has cured, the block is removed from the form, and a short length of 2 x 4-in. stock drilled and fastened to the block by means of the bolt. The trellis is then nailed or screwed to the 2 x 4, using either galvanized roofing nails or brass screws.

— FOLDING BACKYARD TRELLIS —

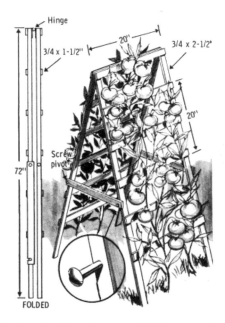

This folding backyard trellis suitable for climbing beans, peas, tomatoes and other vegetables is easy to make from scrap lumber, and takes little storage space. See the illustration for details of its construction.

BUILD a POOL
in Your Garden

4" CONCRETE

CHICKEN WIRE

VALVE IN DRAIN TILE

SOIL

SOIL BOXES

6" GRAVEL

6" CONCRETE

REINFORCING No. 40 MESH

SCREENED OUTLET PIPE CAN BE UNSCREWED AT COUPLING IN SUMP FOR COMPLETE DRAINAGE

¾" X 3"

¾" X ¾"

3" X 3"

1" X 3"

11'-0"

26"

CLEAT

½" CARRIAGE BOLTS

7'-6" R.

16"

2" X 6" BAND-SAWED FROM 2" X 10"

— SMALL POOLS ARE INEXPENSIVE AND EASY TO CONSTRUCT —

An informal pool and rock garden is one of the easiest and least expensive methods of improving your home grounds, and you get immediate results—there's no expensive grading, dirt-moving or waiting one or more years for grass, trees or shrubs to develop. Just scoop out a shallow depression in the ground and pour in some concrete. Then place a few rocks and set out appropriate flowers and plants. You can do all the work yourself, and the pool can be as elaborate as you wish. The pools pictured opposite illustrate the two extremes. The one in the upper right-hand corner is small and plain, yet attractive, while the one in the lower corner is larger and more formal.

Strong watertight concrete is made easily. Most important is the amount of water used per sack of cement, ranging from 4½ to 5 gals., depending on the moisture content of the aggregate. The correct mix should be plastic enough to hold its shape well, but not crumbly. Average proportions are 1 part cement, 2 parts clean, sharp sand and 2½ to 3 parts gravel. Do not permit newly placed concrete to dry out fast. Protect it for a week or ten days. A covering of burlap or canvas, sprinkled often enough to keep it moist, should be used while the concrete is curing.

The lower center detail of the art opposite illustrates a pool with a waterfall. If your backyard slopes, this is an excellent treatment. For convenience in cleaning, soil for the plants should be put in boxes. These should contain a generous amount of stable manure mixed with the soil. A drain pipe is laid before pouring concrete over the bed of cinders or gravel, the latter being used for drainage and also as a cushion in any heaving due to frost. Recommended reinforcement for pools is 40-lb. steel mesh, but if not available you can use old hog or chicken wire, expanded metal lathe or similar material. Concrete in smaller pools is 4 in. instead of 6 in. thick, and is poured directly into the excavation without cinders or gravel underneath. All pools should be on high ground, if possible, to facilitate draining and prevent heavy rains from washing litter into them.

A small footbridge can be made as indicated in the lower right corner of the art opposite. Arched stringers are band-sawed from 10-in.

stock, and the joints are lapped and bolted, with cleats on the inner sides. Treads should be spaced about ¼ in. apart. The top rail is bent down and screwed to the posts, and a batten rail below is also bent. The end posts are creosoted below ground. The bridge can be painted or stained to suit.

— A Convenient Planter —

Not sure what to do with an unsightly tree stump in your yard? Tack a tin strip around the top of the stump and you have a convenient planter for vines that will hide the stump and add beauty to your yard. In only a few years, the hidden stump will rot and then it will be much easier to remove.

— Rustic Steps —

Rustic steps for a steep embankment are surprisingly easy to make. As shown in the illustration they can be made by nailing short logs to a pair of cedar stringers (use fence rails), then burying the stringers in the slope and filling the space behind each riser with fine gravel.

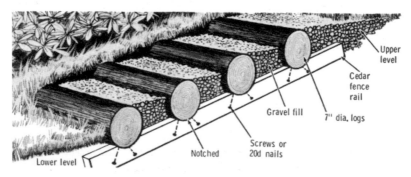

— Coat-Hanger Trellis —

An attractive, expendable trellis can be fashioned from coat hangers in minutes. Fasten the top hanger with hooks or nails in an inverted position and bind each hook with light wire to the hanger below. Partly bury the bottom hanger or stake it to anchor the assembly. This trellis will serve many climbing plants needing but a light support.

— Plants in Hanging Flower Basket Watered Automatically —

Are you going out of town but worried about what will happen to your plants while you're away? With a flowerpot holder made like the one shown, all you need do is fill a reservoir with water, hang the assembly from a hook and plants set in it will be watered automatically.

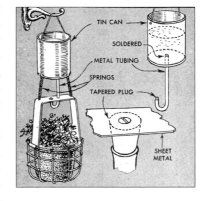

The assembly consists of a tin-can reservoir, a filler tube, a flat-iron strap, two coil springs and a wire basket. The can is punctured in the center where the tube, bent as shown in the right-hand detail, is soldered. The tube is flared to fit over a hardwood plug screwed to the strap, and it is inserted through the latter, to which the basket is attached. The strap is held to the reservoir by the springs as shown. When water evaporates from the pot, the decreased weight permits the springs to raise the basket and strap so that the plug is lifted slightly from the filler tube to allow water to drip into the basket.

— SELF-CLOSING GATE —

This gate is suspended from a horizontal bar by chains, and swings freely about a 1-in. gas pipe, placed vertically in the center of the gate. The chains are of the same length, being fastened equidistant from the pipe, the upper ends farther out than the lower. The distance depends on the weight of the gate and the desired force with which it should close. Any of the numerous styles of latches can be used, if desired.

THE GATE WILL SWING IN EITHER DIRECTION AND COME TO A REST WHERE IT CLOSES THE OPENING.

CHAPTER 3

LOUNGE-ABOUT PROJECTS *for the* PATIO *and* BACKYARD

LOUNGING *in* STYLE

— FOLDING BED CONVERTED TO ATTRACTIVE PATIO LOUNGE CHAIR —

Instead of junking an old folding bed that was no longer being used, one craftsman converted it into an attractive patio lounge chair, shown above, by merely fastening wooden slats over the springs. The link-spring construction of this type of folding bed is a network of wire suspended from the frame by coil springs spaced around the edge. The ½ x 3-in. slats were cut just long enough to stay inside the coil springs. Holes were drilled near the ends of the slats and ¼-in. machine screws were used to hold the slats to the wire. The holes were spaced so they came inside the V-shaped wire into which the coil springs hooked. A larger washer straddles the wire vee and holds each slat securely. Both the slats and the steel bed frame then were painted as protection against the weather.

— HOW TO MAKE A PORCH SWING CHAIR —

The materials needed for making this porch swing chair are two pieces of round wood 2½ in. in diameter and 20 in. long, and two pieces 1¼ in. in diameter and 40 in. long. These longer pieces can be made square, but for appearance it is best to have them round or square with corners rounded. A piece of canvas, or other stout cloth, 16 in. wide and 50 in. long, is to be used for the seat. The two short pieces of wood are used for the ends of the chair and two 1-in. holes are bored in each of them, 1½ in. from the ends, and between the holes and the ends grooves are cut around them to make a place to fasten ropes, as shown at *B, Figure 1*. The two longer pieces are used for the sides, and a tenon is cut on each end of them to fit in the 1-in. holes bored in the end pieces, as shown at *A, Figure 1*. The canvas is now tacked on the end pieces and the pieces given one turn before placing the mortising together.

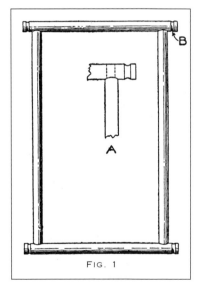

FIG. 1

The chair is now hung up to the porch ceiling with ropes attached to a large screw eye or hook. The end of the chair to be used for the lower part is held about 16 in. from the floor with ropes direct from the grooves in the end pieces to the hook.

The upper end is supported by using a rope in the form of a loop or bail, as shown in *Figure 2*. The middle of the loop or bail should be about 15 in. from the end piece of the chair. Another rope is attached to the loop and through the hook and to a slide as shown. This will allow for adjustment to make the device into a chair or a hammock.

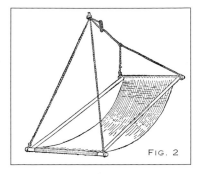

FIG. 2

— FOLDING TABLE AND CHAIRS —

Tea parties galore are in store for the little hostess of your family when she can entertain with this novel table-and-chair set. It is lightweight and folds, so that little tots can carry it easily. Very little material is required to make it.

Figure 5 shows how compactly the table and chairs fold. This is an advantage where space is limited. The set can

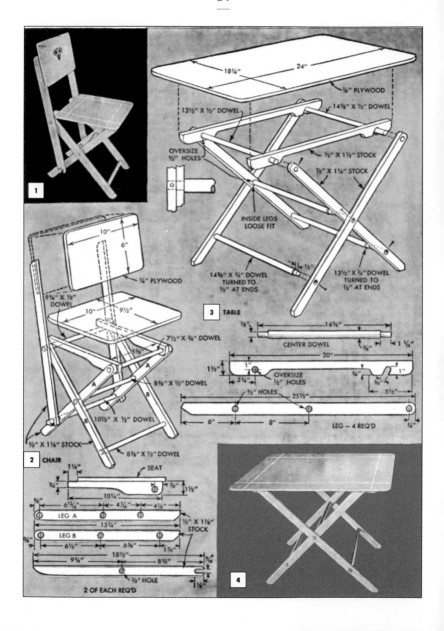

18¼"
24"
¼" PLYWOOD

13½" X ½" DOWEL
14⅜" X ½" DOWEL

OVERSIZE
½" HOLES

½" X 1½" STOCK
½" X 1¼" STOCK

INSIDE LEGS
LOOSE FIT

14⅜" X ¾" DOWEL
TURNED TO
½" AT ENDS

13½" X ¾" DOWEL
TURNED TO
½" AT ENDS

½"

1

3 TABLE

½"
14⅜"
CENTER DOWEL
¾"
1 ¼"

20"
1½"
1"
OVERSIZE
½" HOLES
2¾"
¾"
¾"
1"
5½"

½" HOLES
25½"

6"
8"
LEG — 4 REQ'D
¾"

10"
6"
¼" PLYWOOD

9¾" X ½"
DOWEL

10"
9½"

7½" X ¾" DOWEL

5⅜"

8⅝" X ½" DOWEL

A
A
B
B

10½" X ½" DOWEL

½" X 1⅛" STOCK

8⅝" X ½" DOWEL

2 CHAIR

1⅛"
SEAT
¾"
⅞"
1½"
10¼"
⅝"
6¹³⁄₁₆"
4¹⁄₁₆"
4¼"
LEG A
½" X 1⅛"
STOCK
15¾"
¾"
6½"
6⅜"
1⅞"
LEG B
18½"
9¾"
8¾"
⁵⁄₁₆"
½" HOLE
1⅛"

2 OF EACH REQ'D

4

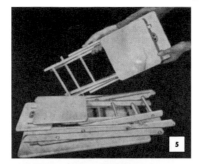

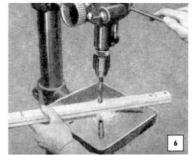

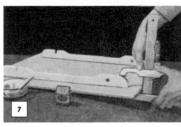

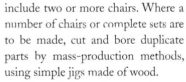

include two or more chairs. Where a number of chairs or complete sets are to be made, cut and bore duplicate parts by mass-production methods, using simple jigs made of wood.

The chairs: Any number of chairs can be made. Several duplicate parts can be cut and drilled at one time, *Figure 6,* and if power tools are available, a setup can be used to mass-produce the parts quickly and uniformly. *Figure 2* details the assembly of the chair and the plan below it gives the size of the members comprising the framework. Note that the stretches are standard dowel stock and are purchased ready-made.

With the exception of the seat board and back rest, which are plywood, all parts are of ½-in. stock. Leg and back members are 1⅛ in. wide, while the seat supports are shaped from stock 1½ in. wide. Notice that the ends of the stretchers fit flush with the outside faces of the legs and that the lower rear one extends through the back legs about ⅞ in. at each end, over which the notched back members hook.

Except where the parts pivot, all stretcher holes should be bored for a light press fit, the others being made slightly oversize. In the latter case, the holes can be enlarged for a sliding fit with a round file or sandpaper wrapped around a smaller dowel. In assembling the parts, allow sufficient clearance between the joints. It's a good idea to use a metal or cardboard washer to prevent rubbing of the painted surfaces. Nails are driven crosswise through the legs and into the stretchers where indicated.

The table: Construction of the table is similar to the chairs. *Figure 3* shows how it goes together, and also gives the size of the parts required. Note that the stretchers are turned down at the ends to fit ½-in. holes in the legs. This adds rigidity, but, if desired, you can simply drive them into undersize holes and pin them. The top and its underframing must be ready for assembly at the same time as the other parts. *Figure 7* shows how to clamp the underframing to the tabletop. The holes in which the top pivots are made oversize, and the notches at the opposite end are formed by first drilling ⅝-in. holes and then sawing in from the edge at an angle to meet the holes.

Finishing: The parts can be painted easily if done before assembly. Check to see that the chairs and table fold freely and then dismantle for finishing. Spray equipment turns the job into play and permits use of quick-drying lacquer. Give all the parts a coat of lacquer sealer first and, when dry, sand them lightly. Then finish with a couple coats of lacquer. Brushing lacquer is available but it requires considerable experience to apply. Very little brushing can be done and the lacquer must be applied with full brush loads in a sweeping motion to avoid lap marks. Enamel, perhaps, is the best to use with a brush. The original set was done in light blue and striped in white as shown in *Figures 1* and *4*.

— HOW TO MAKE A RUSTIC SEAT —

The rustic settee illustrated in *Figure 1* may be made 6 ft. long, which will accommodate four average-sized persons. It is not advisable to exceed this length, as then it would look out of proportion. Select the material for the posts, and for preference branches that are slightly curved, as shown in the sketch. The front posts are about 3½ in. in diameter by 2 ft. 4 in. long. The back posts are 3 ft. 4 in. high, while the center post is

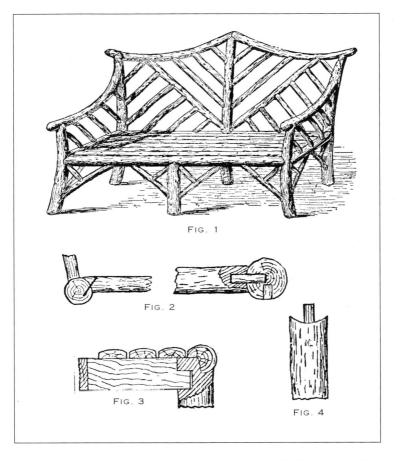

FIG. 1

FIG. 2

FIG. 3

FIG. 4

3 ft. 8 in. in height. The longitudinal and transverse rails are about 3 in. in diameter and their ends are pared away to fit the post to which they are connected by 1-in. diameter dowels. This method is shown in *Figure 4*. The dowel holes are bored at a distance of 1 ft. 2½ in. up from the lower ends of the posts. The front center leg is partially halved to the front rail and also connected to the back post by a bearer, 4 in. deep by 1½ in. thick. This bearer is tenoned to the back post.

Figure 3 shows a sectional view of the bearer joint to front leg, the half-round seat battens resting on the bearer, and also them with their edges planed. It is advisable to have a space between the edges of each batten, say about ⅛ in., to allow rainwater to drain. The ends of the seat battens are pared away to fit the transverse rails neatly, as shown in *Figure 2*. The struts for the post range in diameter from 1½ in. to 2 in. The ends of the struts are pared to fit the posts and

rails, and are then secured with two or three brads at each end.

Select curved pieces, about 2½ in. in diameter, for the arm rests and back rails; meanwhile the diagonally placed filling may be about 2 in. in diameter. Start with the shortest lengths, cutting them longer than required, as the paring necessary to fit them to the rails and posts shortens them a little. Brad them in position as they are fitted, and try to arrange them at regular intervals.

— BARREL-STAVE HAMMOCK —

A hammock made of barrel staves is more comfortable than one would think, considering the nature of the material employed in making it. Good smooth staves should be selected for this purpose, and if one cares to go to a little trouble, a thor-

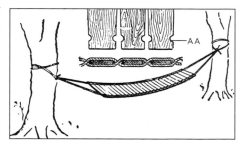

ough sandpapering will make a great improvement. Cut half circles out of

each stave, as shown at *AA*, and pass ropes around.

— WHEELBARROW CHAIR FOR YOUR GARDEN —

R esiliency in the seats of this chair and the footrest to match is obtained by using helical springs to suspend the canvas bottom between

cross members. All the parts are fastened together with screws, although resin glue will give still greater strength. See following illustrations for details.

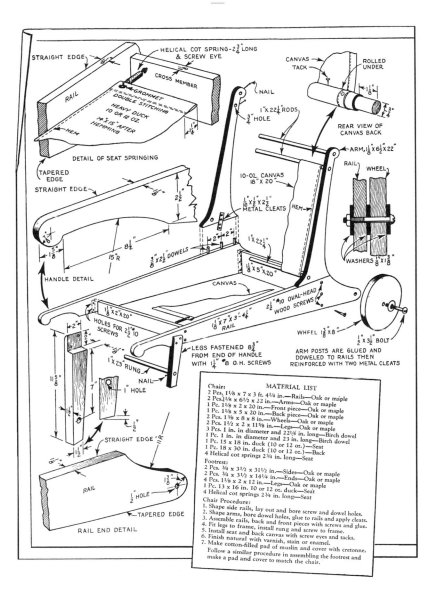

STRAIGHT EDGE

HELICAL COT SPRING-2¾" LONG
& SCREW EYE

CANVAS
TACK

ROLLED
UNDER

RAIL

CROSS MEMBER

⅛"

GROMMET
DOUBLE STITCHING
HEAVY DUCK
10 OR 12 OZ.
¼" X 15" AFTER
HEMMING

NAIL

3¾"

HEM

2½"

¾" HOLE

1" X 22¾" RODS

REAR VIEW OF
CANVAS BACK

DETAIL OF SEAT SPRINGING

ARM, 1⅛" X 6½" X 22"

TAPERED
EDGE

STRAIGHT EDGE

10-OZ. CANVAS
18" X 20

RAIL

WHEEL

1"
2½"

⅝"

HEM

1/10" X ⅛" X 2½"
METAL CLEATS

1" X 22¾"

5⅝"

15" R

8½"

⅜" X 2½" DOWELS

2" 2"

1⅛" X 5" X 20"

WASHERS ⅝" X 1⅛"

HANDLE DETAIL

CANVAS

1⅛" X 2" X 20"

HOLES FOR 2½" 10
SCREWS

2½" #10 OVAL-HEAD
WOOD SCREWS

1⅛" X 7" X 3' 4¼"
RAIL

1" X 23" RUNG

NAIL

1" HOLE

LEGS FASTENED 8¾"
FROM END OF HANDLE
WITH 1¼" #8 O.H. SCREWS

WHEEL 1⅜" X 8"

⅜" X 3½" BOLT

ARM POSTS ARE GLUED AND
DOWELED TO RAILS THEN
REINFORCED WITH TWO METAL CLEATS

2"

11⅝"

7"

½"

STRAIGHT EDGE

1½"

⅛" R

RAIL

½" HOLE

TAPERED EDGE

RAIL END DETAIL

1½"

MATERIAL LIST

Chair:
2 Pcs. 1⅛ x 7 x 3 ft. 4¼ in.—Rails—Oak or maple
2 Pcs. 1⅛ x 6½ x 22 in.—Arms—Oak or maple
1 Pc. 1⅛ x 2 x 20 in.—Front piece—Oak or maple
1 Pc. 1⅛ x 5 x 20 in.—Back piece—Oak or maple
2 Pcs. 1⅜ x 8 x 8 in.—Wheels—Oak or maple
2 Pcs. 1½ x 2 x 11⅝ in.—Legs—Oak or maple
3 Pcs. 1 in. in diameter and 22¼ in. long—Birch dowel
1 Pc. 1 in. in diameter and 23 in. long—Birch dowel
1 Pc. 15 x 18 in. duck (10 or 12 oz.)—Seat
1 Pc. 18 x 30 in. duck (10 or 12 oz.)—Back
4 Helical cot springs 2¾ in. long—Seat

Footrest:
2 Pcs. ¾ x 3½ x 31½ in.—Sides—Oak or maple
2 Pcs. ¾ x 3½ x 14¼ in.—Ends—Oak or maple
4 Pcs. 1⅛ x 2 x 12 in.—Legs—Oak or maple
1 Pc. 13 x 16 in. 10 or 12 oz. duck—Seat
4 Helical cot springs 2¾ in. long—Seat

Chair Procedure:
1. Shape side rails, lay out and bore screw and dowel holes.
2. Shape arms, bore dowel holes, glue to rails and apply cleats.
3. Assemble rails, back and front pieces with screws and glue.
4. Fit legs to frame, install rung and screw to frame.
5. Install seat and back canvas with screw eyes and tacks.
6. Finish natural with varnish, stain or enamel.
7. Make cotton-filled pad of muslin and cover with cretonne.
Follow a similar procedure in assembling the footrest and
make a pad and cover to match the chair.

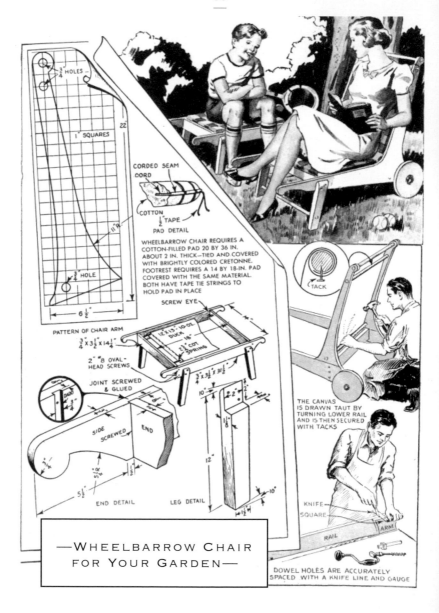

HOLES — 3/4"

1" SQUARES

22

11" R

3/4" HOLE

6 1/2"

PATTERN OF CHAIR ARM

3/4" X 3 1/2" X 14 1/4"

2" #8 OVAL-HEAD SCREWS

CORDED SEAM
CORD

COTTON
1/2" TAPE
PAD DETAIL

WHEELBARROW CHAIR REQUIRES A
COTTON-FILLED PAD 20 BY 36 IN.
ABOUT 2 IN. THICK—TIED AND COVERED
WITH BRIGHTLY COLORED CRETONNE.
FOOTREST REQUIRES A 14 BY 18-IN. PAD
COVERED WITH THE SAME MATERIAL.
BOTH HAVE TAPE TIE STRINGS TO
HOLD PAD IN PLACE

SCREW EYE

12 X 13 10-OZ DUCK
18"
2 1/2" COT SPRING

3/4" X 3 1/2" X 3 1/2"

JOINT SCREWED
& GLUED

DADO

SIDE SCREWED

END

END DETAIL

5 1/2"
5 1/2" R

10"

2"

12"

10"

1 1/2"

LEG DETAIL

TACK

THE CANVAS
IS DRAWN TAUT BY
TURNING LOWER RAIL
AND IS THEN SECURED
WITH TACKS

KNIFE

SQUARE

RAIL   ARM

DOWEL HOLES ARE ACCURATELY
SPACED WITH A KNIFE LINE AND GAUGE

—WHEELBARROW CHAIR
FOR YOUR GARDEN—

STAYING OUT *of the* ELEMENTS

— QUICKLY MADE LAWN TENT —

LAWN TENT COMPLETE.

A very simple way of erecting a lawn tent for the children is to take a large umbrella, such as used on delivery wagons, and drive the handle into the ground deep enough to hold it solid. Fasten canvas or cotton cloth to the ends of the ribs and let it hang so that the bottom edge will touch the ground. Light ropes can be tied to the ends of the ribs and fastened to stakes driven in the ground in a tent-like manner to make the whole more substantial and to stand against a heavy wind. This makes an exceptionally fine tent, as the umbrella is waterproof; also, there is more room to stand up than in a tent that is in the shape of a wigwam.

— ATTRACTIVE PATIO STAND FOR BEACH UMBRELLA —

Here is a portable stand to hold a beach umbrella on a patio or lawn, as well as at the beach. Made from a 5-gal. paint pail, a length of pipe and two pipe fittings, it will hold an average-size umbrella in all but the strongest breeze.

To make it, bolt a 1½-in. pipe flange to bottom of the pail and cut a 2-in. hole in the center of the cover, as shown in the detail. Then screw a 13-in. length of pipe into the flange, fill pail with sand and fasten lid in place. A coupling screwed on the upper end of the pipe holds the stand rigidly together and conceals the cover hole. Paint the stand as desired and apply decals to the sides to give it an attractive appearance. Leave the handle in place for easy carrying.

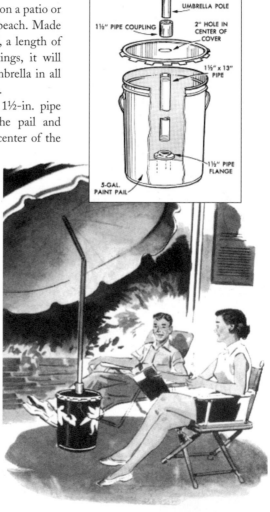

— A-FRAME SIMPLICITY IDEAL
FOR DOG HOUSE —

SHEET-METAL RAIN CAP

VENT HOLES

T-HINGE

½" EXTERIOR PLYWOOD

The roof-wall A-frame construction that makes vacation cabins so quick and easy to erect gives an extra bonus when applied to a home for your pooch: It makes cleaning a cinch. You just drop the hinged sides flat for a quick hosing and airing.

No dimensions are shown on the plans because the design is readily adaptable to any size dog. For an average house pet, an 11-in. square opening in a 32-in. equilateral triangle is ample. You'll then be able to cut both ends and both sides from a single 4 x 8-ft. sheet of ½-in. exterior-grade plywood. You'll need an extra piece, 30¾ x 36 in., for the floor, plus 1 x 4s for the base cleats and cross brace.

All panels should be painted inside and out. No hooks are needed to hold the sides up—the snug-fitting rain cap (which could also be of wood) secures them and seals the ridge slit against rain.

— A Dry Spot on a Rainy Day —

It often occurs when out pic-nicking that a little rain shower spoils the day, even if it does no more than soak the grass and prevent the party from sitting down on it.

The shower need not, however, affect the picnic at all if a piece of heavy canvas is suspended between trees in the manner illustrated, so that a sort of shelter is provided, under which the grass remains perfectly dry.

The canvas can be any desirable size, and can be conveniently folded up and placed under the back seat of an auto. A brass eyelet is provided at each corner, to take the strain of the rope.

A PIECE OF CANVAS, TIED TO TREES, PROVIDES SHELTER FOR A PICNIC PARTY DURING A SHOWER

— Metal Stake for Use in Rocky Ground Supports Tent or Umbrella —

Anyone who frequently has to support a large umbrella, or set up a tent on rocky ground, will find this stake is just the thing. It has a socket welded near one end to take a tent pole or an umbrella standard. It consists of a length of pipe pointed at one end and fitted with a cap at the other to keep the metal from being flared and broken by hammer blows.

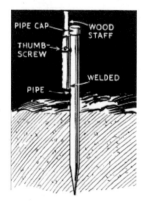

GETTING *in* TOUCH *with the* ELEMENTS

— MIDGET ACROBAT ON TOY WINDMILL CUTS AMUSING CAPERS —

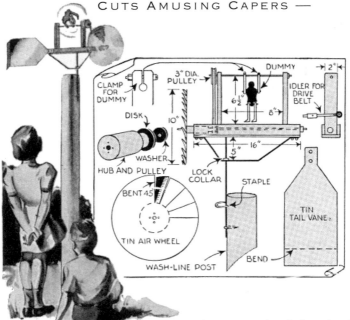

Actuating a trapeze performer in a realistic manner, this wind toy will afford you many laughs, especially on a gusty day when the mill runs erratically. First get a base for the assembly, which can be a piece of hardwood or light channel iron. Fasten vertical pieces

to it to carry the shaft and pulley that rotate the figure. Then provide simple bearings on the base for the airwheel shaft, which is a length of brass rod. Next make up the wheel hub and pulley from hardwood, and drill it to take the shaft with a force fit, placing a washer between the hub and shaft bearing to prevent binding. Now you are ready for the wheel, which is a tin disk cut to resemble the wheel on a regular farm windmill. This is tacked to the hub. A tin tail vane is fastened to the rear of the base. Arms and legs of the figure are pivoted loosely to the body, while the arms are clamped tightly to the shaft.

— A MUSICAL WINDMILL —

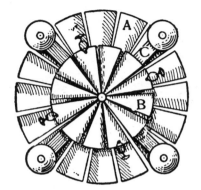

Make two wheels out of tin. They may be of any size, but wheel *A* must be larger than wheel *B*. On wheel *A* fasten two pieces of wood, *C,* to cross in the center, and place a bell on each of the four ends, as shown. The smaller wheel, *B,* must be separated from the other with a round piece of wood or an old spool. Tie four buttons with split rings to the smaller wheel, *B.* The blades on the wheels should be bent opposite on one wheel from the others so as to make the wheels turn in different directions. When turning, the buttons will strike the bells and make them ring constantly.

— A MONOPLANE WEATHER VANE —

The toy windmill or weather vane shown in the sketch is made to represent a Blériot monoplane. The propeller is turned by the wind. The frame is made of heavy wire and connected with straps of tin. The construction is plainly shown in the illustration. The windmill vane can be made in any size to suit the builder.

WIRE AND SHEET-METAL VANE.

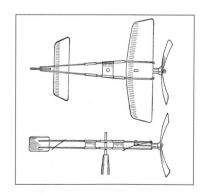

— BUILD YOUR OWN SUNDIAL —

For a center of interest in the garden or terrace, or as a decorative fill-in for a blank spot on the house, design and build a sundial. Bringing something out of the past and displaying it in a modern setting always appeals to the homeowner who wants her home to be distinctive. The sundial, with its historical significance and unusual decorative qualities, is ideal for this purpose.

Actual construction of a sundial is not complicated and permits the use of almost any material that will withstand exposure to the elements. The dial may be cut from lead, copper or linoleum and mounted on a wooden, steel or concrete pedestal, or installed vertically on a wall, or a horizontal dial may be impressed in fresh concrete, laid out in mosaic or even planted in flowers. Thus, you have an almost unlimited range of materials, designs and sizes.

The most important factor in making a sundial that really works is laying out the dial itself. This will vary according to the particular latitude of your home and its longitude in relation to the standard-time meridian. You'll probably want to incorporate the necessary correction in the dial to make its reading agree as nearly as possible with local time.

Before beginning actual selection and layout of a sundial, it is best to understand the principles on which a sundial functions. These are best explained by the equatorial dial so named because the dial plate is in the same plane as the earth's equator. This is the simplest type of dial and the one on which all other dials are based. The gnomon, a thin rod that casts a shadow on the plate of the equatorial dial, works in the same way as a flagstaff at the north pole; that is, as the earth revolves, the summer sun would cast the shadow of the flagstaff through a full circle each 24-hr. period. As the circle is 360 deg., each 15-deg. segment of the circle is equivalent to 1 hr. The equatorial dial is easily made, as shown in the details of *Figure 3,* and will give you an accurate reading. Its one objection, however, is that it will

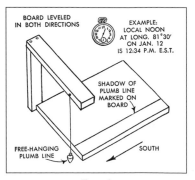

FIG. 2

only tell time from March to September in the northern hemisphere. The horizontal and declining vertical dials are a little more complicated, but they will tell time the year 'round.

There are two corrections necessary to permit your sundial to indicate time accurately. One is the daily correction to allow for the variation of length of the actual day with that of the 24-hr. day used by civil time. This variation reaches a maximum of 16 min., as indicated by the table, opposite. If you desire, a scale for making this correction can be incorporated in the equatorial dial.

The second correction is necessary to make local noon—the time when the sun is due south and at its highest point in the sky—agree with noon according to standard time. The necessity

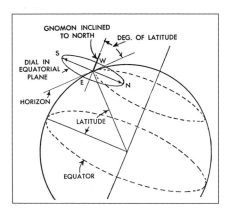

FIG. 1

Date		Minutes	Date		Minutes
Jan.	1–6	+4	Aug.	1–4	+8
	7–16	+8		5–25	+4
	17–31	+12		26–31	0
Feb.	1–29	+14	Sept.	1–7	0
March	1–11	+12		8–18	-4
	12–25	+8		19–30	-8
	26–31	+4	Oct.	1–14	-12
April	1–7	+4		15–31	-16
	8–25	0	Nov.	1–21	-16
	26–30	-4		22–30	-12
May	1–31	-4	Dec.	1–3	-12
June	1–3	-4		4–12	-8
	4–23	0		13–21	-4
	24–30	+4		22–28	0
July	1–16	+4		29–31	+4
	17–31	+8			

DAILY CORRECTION TABLE.

for this becomes obvious when you take into consideration the fact that standard-time zones are based on the sun, or local, time at the nearest meridian. So, unless you live right on a meridian, the sun time shown on the dial will be slow if west of the meridian or fast if east of that line. To compensate for the difference in time, find your location on a map to the nearest half deg. (30 min.) of longitude. Then determine the difference between your longitude and that of your standard-time meridian. Each deg. of difference equals 4 min. variation in time. Thus, if you are 3 deg. west of the time meridian, 12 min. would be added to the dial time to obtain standard time. If you are the same distance east of the meridian, you would subtract 12 min. This correction remains the same throughout the year and may be incorporated permanently into the sundial.

Your time zone is determined by the following meridians: Eastern Standard Time, 75 deg. W.; Central Standard Time, 90 deg. W.; Mountain Standard Time, 105 deg. W.; Pacific Standard Time, 120 deg. W.

The easiest method of finding the local noon line, which is the basis of the sundial, is shown in *Figure 2*. First find the standard-time correction, as mentioned in the preceding paragraph, and check with the table to find the daily correction. Then set your watch accurately. The next step is to set up a board and free-hanging plumb line, *Figure 2*, in the location in which you will set up the sundial. The shadow cast on the board by the plumb line will indicate local noon when the time on your watch reads noon plus or minus the two corrections. Note the example in *Figure 2*.

Layout and construction of an equatorial sundial are detailed in *Figure 3*. As in the upper detail, the noon line is established first and the hour lines are laid out at 15-deg. intervals in both directions from the noon line. Each hour is divided into 15-min. segments, which, in turn, are marked off in 5-min. divisions. If

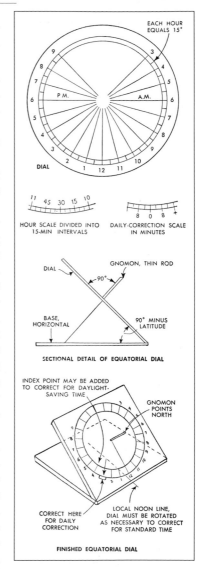

FIG. 3

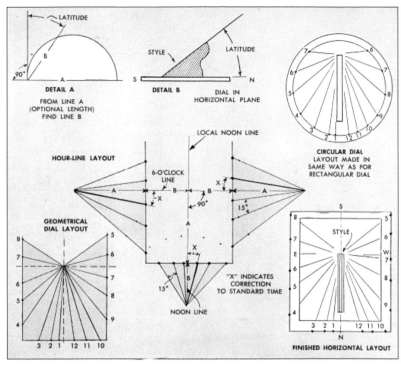

FIG. 4

the dial plate is mounted slightly, a daily correction scale may be marked just outside the face of the dial and the dial plate adjusted each day to incorporate the correction. The scale is graduated in 4-min. intervals to indicate a maximum of plus or minus 16 min.

Although the dial can be any diameter desired, a diameter of 7½ in. is convenient. This makes the hour segments about 1 in. long and facilitates marking the minute divisions. The gnomon should be a straight length of thin rod, preferably brass or aluminum, mounted vertically in the center of the dial.

The leveled board which you used to find the local noon line can be used as a base for the dial, or a replacement base can be made of more substantial material. This, of course, must be located and marked carefully to be sure that it is level in both directions and that the position of the local noon line is accurate. As shown in the lower detail of *Figure 3*, the noon line on the dial should be aligned with the local noon line, with the gnomon pointing north. The angle of the dial plate to the base, which is horizontal, should be 90 deg. minus the deg. of latitude. Note that this corresponds with the diagram in *Figure 1*. If carefully installed and properly calibrated, the dial can be expected to tell time within a range of about 2 min., plus or minus.

Of the several types of sundials which tell time throughout the year, the horizontal dial is the most popular and is frequently seen mounted on top of a concrete column in the center of a formal garden. A somewhat similar dial, designed for installation on outside wall surfaces, is called a declining vertical dial.

The horizontal dial is detailed in *Figure 4*, the same layout being used whether the shape of the dial plate is round, square, hexagonal or any other geometric pattern. The popular round design mounted on a concrete column is shown in the photo above.

Note in the hour-line layout in *Figure 4* that there are two critical

THIS PHOTO DEPICTS A HORIZONTAL SUNDIAL, A POPULAR CHOICE FOR FORMAL GARDENS.

dimensions involved—the lengths of lines *A* and *B*. The first step is to decide on a length for line *A*, determining it by the size of dial you want to make. Then, as in detail *A*, use line *A* as a diameter and scribe a half circle. From one end of the half circle, lay out a line perpendicular to the base, *A*. Then, using the deg. of latitude as the angle, draw in line *B* from the base of the perpendicular. The length of line *B* is determined by measuring from the base to the point where the line intersects the arc of the half circle.

On the hour-line layout, line *A* becomes a portion of the local noon line. From the upper end of line *A,* line *B* is drawn at right angles on each side. The line *B-B* forms the 6 o'-clock line. Using the ends of line *B-B* and the lower end of line *A* as reference points, draw three sides of a rectangle perpendicular to the reference lines, as shown. Extend both ends of line *B-B* and the lower end of line *A* as reference points, draw three sides of a rectangle perpendicular to the reference lines, as shown. Extend both ends of line *B-B* a distance equal to line *A* to establish a point on both sides of the rectangle for laying out the hour lines. Extend the lower end of vertical line *A* a distance equal to line *B* for laying out the hour lines at the bottom of the rectangle.

The standard-time corrections should be incorporated into the horizontal dial at this stage of the layout. Both the noon line and the two

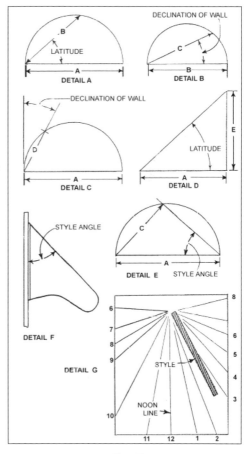

FIG. 5

6 o'-clock lines are moved as indicated by *X* in the detail. The angle *X* is equal to the number of deg. necessary to correct for standard time in your area, as previously mentioned.

In the example in *Figure 4,* the location of the dial is west of the meridian and the time is added. Were the dial east of the meridian, the *X* correction would be made in the opposite direction.

Then, using the relocated noon line and 6 o'-clock lines as bases, draw in lines at 15-deg. intervals. Mark the sides of the rectangle where the lines intersect them. From the upper end of line *A,* at the point where line *B-B* intersects it, draw lines to the marks along the sides of the rectangle. These become the hour lines, as indicated by the geometrical dial layout.

The style is cut out as in detail *B,* its angle being equal to the deg. of latitude. The apex of the style angle points south, or to the top of the layouts shown in the details, and is located at the intersection of lines *A* and *B-B.* The style should be of thin material or both sides of its top edge should be carefully beveled to cast an accurate shadow. The finished style is mounted directly over the local noon line.

The declining vertical dial, detailed in *Figures 5* and *6,* is designed for mounting on any wall that faces in a southerly direction. The angle of declination is the angle that the wall deviates from south. If there were no angle

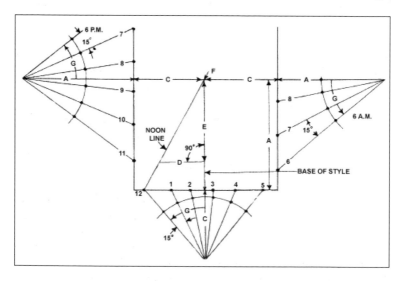

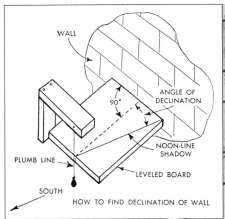

WALL

ANGLE OF
DECLINATION

90°

NOON-LINE
SHADOW

PLUMB LINE

LEVELED BOARD

SOUTH

HOW TO FIND DECLINATION OF WALL

FIG. 7

THIS PHOTO PICTURES A
VERTICAL DECLINING SUNDIAL.
THIS DIAL DECLINES A FEW
DEGREES TOWARD THE EAST
SO BASE OF STYLE FALLS
IN MORNING HOURS.

of declination; that is, if the wall faced directly to the south, the dial would be laid out in almost the same way as a horizontal dial. The only difference between the horizontal and vertical dials, in this case, would be the use of the deg. of latitude when determining line *B*, as in *Figure 5*, detail *A*.

To make the declining vertical dial, it is first necessary to find the angle of declination. This is done as in *Figure 7*, using a leveled board and a plumb line to cast a shadow of the noon line. Use the same method for finding the noon line as that referred to in *Figure 2*, except that in this case the board is mounted against the wall instead of being faced due south. When the noon line shadow is cast on the board, draw in the noon line and draw a line at right angles to the wall to meet the noon line at the outer edge of the board. The angle formed by the noon line and the perpendicular is the angle of declination.

The lengths of the various lines necessary to lay out the declining vertical dial are figured as in the upper details of *Figure 5*. Following the details *A* to *E* in sequence enables you to determine the line lengths for the layout plus the angle of the style. Here again, the optional length of line *A* controls the size of the sundial. First layout line *A* to the decided length, using it as a diameter, and scribe a half circle. Then draw in line *B*, as indicated in detail *A*. After measuring the length of line *B*, use it as a diameter and scribe another half circle. In this case, use the angle of declination to find the length of line *C*, as in detail *B*. To find the length of line *D*, use the half circle having line *A* as its base, and draw in a perpendicular at one end of the base. Then, using the angle of declination, find the length of line *D*, detail *C*. Detail *D* shows how line *A* becomes the base of a right triangle, having the degree of latitude as the known angle, to determine the length of line *E*.

The style angle is determined from lines *A* and *C*, as in detail *E*, and the style itself is made as in detail *F*. The length of the style is optional. The base of the style will be mounted along line *E* so that the apex of the style angle is at point *F*.

After the lengths of the lines have been determined, the layout is made as in *Figure 6*. Approximately the same procedure is used as that for laying out the horizontal drawing line *D* at right angles to the lower end of line *E*. Line *D* is drawn to the left of line *E* for a dial which declines to the west. If the dial declined to the east, as it would if mounted on

the wall in *Figure 7*, line *D* would be added to the right of line *E*.

Line *E* is extended below the bottom of the rectangular layout a distance equal to line *C*. Then a line is drawn between the bottom of line *C* and the end of the noon line. The hour lines, from noon to 5 P.M., are laid out at 15-deg. intervals from this line. At this point, the angle *G* is measured as indicated and transposed to both the right- and left-hand sides of the layout to determine the 6 P.M. and 6 A.M. lines. The standard-time correction also can be added at this time. This is done in the same way as shown in the hour lines in the same manner as for the horizontal dial.

The balance of the hour lines are laid out by using the 6 o'-clock lines as bases. After the hour lines are all drawn to the center point, *F*, the layout is turned to bring the noon line in the vertical position. The finished layout is shown in *Figure 5*, detail *G*.

When mounting the declining vertical dial on a wall, it is best to use a plumb line to be sure that the noon line is vertical. Be sure, however, that in mounting the dial, you do not change the angle of declination. The style should be vertical to the dial plate.

To obtain civil time, add or subtract the number of minutes shown from the reading on the sundial.

— Telescope Stand and Holder —

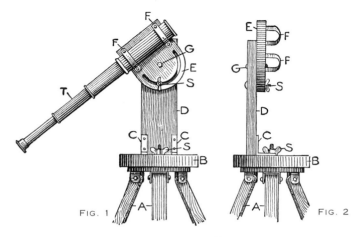

MADE OF A CAMERA TRIPOD.

With the ordinary small telescope it is very difficult to keep the line of sight fixed upon any particular object. To meet the situation, I constructed the device herewith. A circular piece of wood, *B*, 6 in. in diameter, is fastened to a common camera tripod, *A*, with a set screw, *S*. Corner irons, *CC*, are screwed to the circular piece. These corner irons are also screwed to, and supported in a vertical position by, the wood standard *D*, which is 4 in. wide and of any desired height. To this standard is secured the wood shield-shaped piece *E* by the screw *G* upon which it turns. A semicircular slit is cut in the piece *G*,

through which passes the set screw *S*. The telescope is secured to the piece *G* by means of the pipe straps *FF*. Rubber bands are put around the telescope to prevent rubbing at the places where the straps enclose it.

The wood pieces were made of ½-in. mahogany, well rubbed with linseed oil to give them a finish. The corner irons and set screws or bolts with thumb-nuts can be purchased at any hardware store. The pipe straps of different sizes can be obtained from a plumber's or gas and steam fitter's store. With this device, either a vertical or horizontal motion may be secured, and, after bringing the desired object into the line of sight, the set screws will hold the telescope in position. Anyone owning a tripod can construct this device in three or four hours' time at a trifling cost. In *Figure 1* is shown the side view of the holder and stand, and *Figure 2* the front view. It may be of interest to those owning telescopes without eyepieces to know that such an eyepiece can be obtained very cheaply by purchasing a pair of colored eyeglasses with very dark lenses and metal rims. Break off the frame, leaving the metal rims and nibs at each end. Place these over the eyepiece of the telescope and secure in place with rubber bands looped over the nibs and around the barrel of the instrument.

—A *Popular Mechanics* reader

— TIPPING BIRDBATH ATTRACTS SONGBIRDS AND KEEPS CATS AWAY —

If you want to put a birdbath in your yard to attract songbirds, and at the same time save the birds from being molested by prowling cats, this tipping birdbath will serve both purposes. A 5-ft. length of soil pipe is set in the ground so that 3 ft. of it projects above the surface. The bowl of the bath, which is a cover from a garbage can, is held on the base by a sash weight tied to the handle and suspended inside the soil pipe. When a cat attempts to get at birds in the bath, the cover tips and spills water on him. The sudden loss of support, plus the water bath, will discourage even the most persistent cat. The cover will right itself as soon as the weight is removed, because of

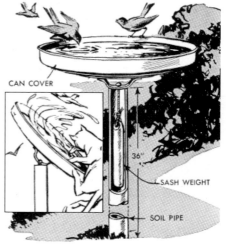

CAN COVER

36"

SASH WEIGHT

SOIL PIPE

the sash weight. The soil pipe and garbage-can cover could be painted a bright color, or stones and colored bits of pottery might be cemented around the soil pipe as decoration.

— Pheasant Feeders from Milk Cans Keep Out All Rodents —

Used by a Wisconsin gun club, this self-feeder for pheasants and other game birds is made from an old milk can. Supported from a tree limb by means of two wires, the can is held above the ground so that rabbits and other rodents cannot reach it. Tabs are cut around the can near the bottom and then pushed inward to provide the feed openings. A number of holes drilled around the upper rim of the can provide air vents to keep the grain from accumulating moisture and freezing.

— Bird Feeder from Mixing Bowls —

Here is a simple bird feeder that anyone can make with a little work. It consists of two wooden mixing bowls, one about 2 in. larger than the other, and a length of large dowel. Three drain holes are drilled in the smaller bowl, after which both bowls are attached to the ends of the dowel with screw eyes, as shown. The feeder can be suspended between two tree branches.

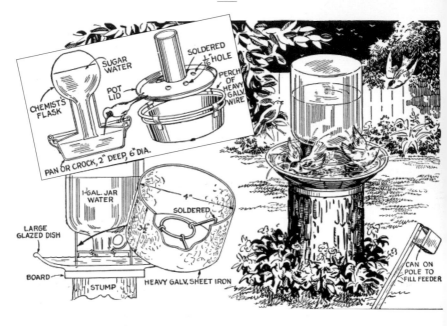

— KEEPING THE BIRDS AT HOME IN YOUR GARDEN —

Chances of attracting birds and keeping them around are increased if you will provide water which is readily accessible to them. Where water quickly evaporates from a shallow dish, a constant supply can be maintained by using inverted flasks or jugs held a short distance above the bottom of the pans or dishes as shown in the pictures above.

Take the simple type of birdbath shown in the above illustration, at the far right: A large, shallow dish, preferably light green in color, is set on a stump or pedestal and a gallon jug of water, fitted with a sheet-metal collar, is placed inverted in the center of the dish. The collar is wide enough to keep the mouth of the jug above the bottom and a wire frame in the collar serves to hold the jug in position securely. The result is a constant supply of water until the jug is empty.

The same principle is used in making the small sugar-water feeder shown at the upper left. In this case, a flask or bottle is used as the reservoir while the pan is covered with a perforated cover to minimize evaporation. The cover should be located just above the level of the liquid so that birds will have no difficulty in getting at it. A California bird lover succeeded in attracting hundreds of humming-birds to his ground by using such feeders. For humming-birds, the feeder should be arranged so that they have access to the liquid while on the wing as they seldom alight.

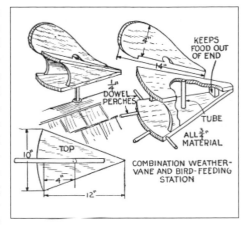

KEEPS FOOD OUT OF END

DOWEL PERCHES

TUBE

ALL ¾" MATERIAL

TOP

COMBINATION WEATHER-VANE AND BIRD-FEEDING STATION

The lower detail of the illustration shows a protected feeding shelter in which crumbs can be placed. The shelter is pivoted to rotate and the vane on top keeps it pointed into the wind. Keeping the feeder supplied with crumbs is easy if you use a long stick or pole having a can nailed to the top end.

— ENTRANCE OF BEEHIVE ADJUSTED BY STICK TO SUIT WEATHER —

To reduce the entrance of snow and sleet into his beehive, without restraining the bees from their necessary cleaning flights, one keeper uses square sticks, which fit easily into the entrance opening. Each stick is slotted on two sides, as indicated, to produce large or small doorways. The sticks are adjusted to bring either size of notch into use as the weather demands.

BEEHIVE

NOTCHED STICK

— HOW TO CHAIN A DOG —

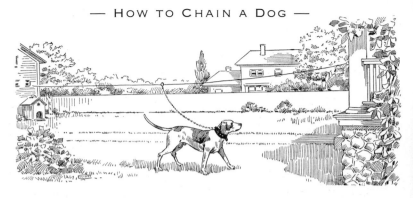

A good way to chain a dog and give him plenty of exercise is to stretch a clothesline or a galvanized wire between the house and barn on which is placed a ring large enough to slide freely. The chain from the dog's collar is fastened to the ring. This method can also be used for tethering a cow or horse, the advantage being the use of a short tie rope eliminating the possibility of the animal becoming entangled.

TIME *for a* PICNIC

— JUMP SEAT FOR A CHILD —

Jump seats for small "freeloaders" are easily added at the ends of a standard woodframe picnic table. Place 2 x 6s edgewise under the table, long enough to support the end seats. Nail to the *X*-legs and toe-nail to the regular seat supports. Then cut two short lengths from a 1 x 12 board, and them nail to the projecting ends.

— CHILDREN'S PICNIC TABLE HAS ADJUSTABLE SEATS —

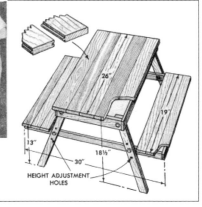

Durable, good looking and light enough to be moved about easily, this picnic table for children can be used indoors or out. It is built of lengths of scrap hardwood flooring and is assembled with bolts through the legs and framing, the tongue-and-grooved top being attached with screws. Holes drilled in the legs permit the seats to be adjusted for height. The table can be stained or left natural, but spar varnish should be applied to protect it from moisture if it is to be used outdoors.

— MAKESHIFT HEADREST —

A jury rig for holding a headrest pillow in place on the back of a wooden lawn chair, as shown, is two spring-type clothespins screwed to the back of a chair. To provide screwdriver clearance, one leg of the clothespin may be forced aside temporarily, or a hole can be drilled in it as detailed. Use sheet-metal screws on a metal chair.

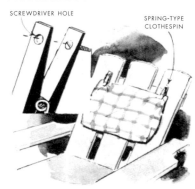

— KEEP YOUR FOOD COOL —

A packaged ice cake which will last a long time in your picnic chest can be made by freezing water in one or two half-gallon milk cartons. Water from the melting ice will remain in the cartons so that food placed in the bottom of the chest won't be water-soaked.

— PICNIC SALT AND PEPPER SHAKERS —

Picnic meals call for salt, and finding a container is no problem if you hang on to an empty spice box. The kind with the sliding metal top is ideal since it is lightweight, leakproof and unbreakable.

Individual salt and pepper shakers, handy for traveling and for picnics, can also be made from dental-floss containers. Turn back the metal hook on the top of the container and pinch five to seven additional holes in it. After the containers are filled, place a paper or cork disk under the cap to prevent spilling while in transit. Remove this disk and the little shaker is ready for use.

— KEEP PICNIC CLOTH FROM BLOWING AWAY —

Picnic luncheon cloths won't be blown away when the first gentle breeze makes an appearance if you anchor each corner firmly to the ground with a large cotter pin. Attach each cotter pin to the cloth with a safety pin. For added convenience, complete the installation before the cloths are packed. Then just drive the pins into the ground.

— ✻ ✻ ✻ —

{ CHAPTER 4 }

THE SPORTING GIRL MAKES *a* SPLASH

DIVE IN

— A CONCRETE SWIMMING POOL —

Several youngsters from a neighborhood in the suburbs of a large city concluded to make for themselves a swimming tank of concrete. The money was raised by various means to purchase the cement, and the work was done by themselves. The ground was selected in a secluded spot in a neighbor's backyard and a hole dug to a depth of 4 ft., 12 ft. wide and

22 ft. long. The concrete was made by mixing 1 part cement, 4 parts sand and 10 parts gravel together and the bulk moistened with water. The bottom was made the same as layering a sidewalk, and forms were only used for the inside of the surrounding wall. The tank may be hidden with shrubbery or vines planted to grow over a poultry wire fence.

— NON-SLIP DIVING BOARD —

RUBBER BANDS

The slippery surface of a wet diving board is often the cause of injury to swimmers, so the manager of a lake resort devised a very simple and practical method for making the boards at his beach slip-proof. A number of rubber bands, about 2 in. wide, were cut from discarded inner tubes and snapped over the board, spaced about 1 in. apart. Happily these rubber bands provided enough friction for the divers' feet to prevent them from slipping, even when attempting more complicated dives off the board.

— DIVING TOWER FOR THE SUMMER CAMP —

Aquatic pleasures and sports at a summer camp or lake may be considerably enlivened by the building of a diving tower like that shown in the sketch. It has proved very successful at a summer camp at Crystal Lake, Illinois. The youngsters have made a practice for several years of building a tower early each swimming season on the opening of their camp in July and disposing of it at the close of camp some weeks later. Several resorts and cottages now boast towers made by the campers.

The tower is built largely of 2 x 4-in. stock. The longer pieces at the corners are 12 ft. in length, slanted so that the lower end of the tower is 7 ft. square and the platform at the top 3 ft. square. The handrail at the top is fixed to extensions of the rear uprights.

A springboard is fastened on two horizontal braces near the middle of the tower and is reached by the ladder. The structure is built on the

STONE

CHILDREN AT A SUMMER CAMP CONSTRUCT A DIVING TOWER EACH SUMMER AND DISPOSE OF IT FOR THE COST OF LUMBER WHEN THEY BREAK CAMP. THE TOWER IS BUILT LARGELY OF 2 X 4-IN. STOCK AND IS WEIGHTED WITH A BOX OF STONES.

shore and towed out to its position. It is sunk and weighted by the box of stones supported on cross braces.

— HOW TO MAKE WATER WINGS —

Purchase a piece of unbleached muslin, 1 yd. square. Take this and fold it over once, forming a double piece 1½ ft. wide and 3 ft. long. Make a double stitch all around the edge, leaving a small opening at one corner. Insert a piece of tape at this corner to be used for tying around the opening when the bag is blown up. The bag is then turned inside out, soaked with water and blown up. An occasional wetting all over will prevent it from leaking. As these wings are very large, they will prevent the swimmer from sinking when they need a rest.

THE BOATING LIFE

— KNOW YOUR KNOTS —

Learning how to tie the right knot for each situation is a challenge for the new boater. Before you begin you will need to learn how to whip rope with nylon whipping thread. First, wind the thread over the loop and pass the end through, then pull the loop under the whipping, clip loose ends and heat the whipped section to melt the wax coating and fuse the strands.

You can begin your knot-tying training by learning how to recognize basic knots. On the following page, you'll find a visual glossary of some useful knots every boater should have in his or her repertoire, from bowlines to mooring hitches.

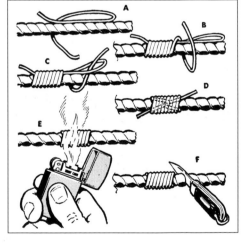

WHIP ROPE WITH NYLON THREAD TO KEEP IT FROM FRAYING.

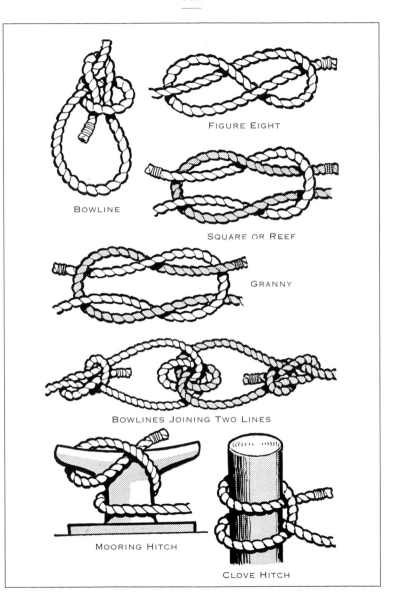

BOWLINE

FIGURE EIGHT

SQUARE OR REEF

GRANNY

BOWLINES JOINING TWO LINES

MOORING HITCH

CLOVE HITCH

— HOMEMADE MARINER'S COMPASS —

You don't have to purchase a mariner's compass; you can make your own. Magnetize an ordinary knitting needle, *A*, and push it through a cork, *B*, and place the cork exactly in the middle of a needle. Thrust a pin, *C*, through the cork at right angles to the needle, and stick two sharpened matches in the sides of the cork so that they will project downward as shown. The whole arrangement is balanced on a thimble with balls of wax stuck on the heads of the matches. If the needle is not

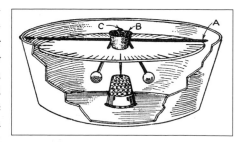

A SIMPLE COMPASS CAN BE MADE FROM A MAGNETIZED KNITTING NEEDLE AND OTHER COMMON ODDS AND ENDS.

horizontal, pull it through the cork to one side or the other, or change the wax balls. The whole device is placed in a glass berry dish and covered with a pane of glass.

— READING A BAROMETER —

Here's how to understand what your barometer is telling you: A falling needle means that a storm is on its way. A fast-rising needle indicates clear, windy weather. Variable or rainy weather is indicated by a steady but slowly falling barometer.

A steady but slowly rising barometer signifies that the weather has settled. If the wind is shifting to the west and the barometer is rising, you can expect fair weather. The combination of an east wind and falling barometer spell bad weather.

— HOW TO MAKE A CRUISING CATAMARAN —

A launch is much safer than a sailing boat, yet there is not the real sport to be derived from it as in sailing. Herein is given a description of a sailing catamaran especially adapted for those who desire to sail

and have a safe craft. The main part of the craft is made from two boats or pontoons with watertight tops, bottoms, and sides and fixed at a certain distance apart with a platform on top for the passengers. Such a craft cannot be capsized easily, and, as the pontoons are watertight, it will weather almost any rough water. If the craft is intended for rough waters, care must be taken to make the platforms pliable yet stiff and as narrow as convenient to take care of the rocking movements.

This catamaran has been designed to simplify the construction, and, if a larger size than the dimensions shown in *Figure 1* is desired, the pontoons may be made longer by using two boards end to end and putting battens on the inside over the joint. Each pontoon is made of two boards

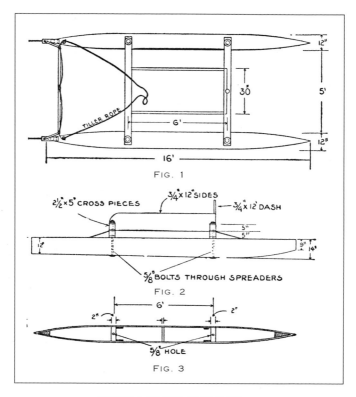

FIG. 1

FIG. 2

FIG. 3

DETAILS OF THE PONTOONS.

1 in. thick, 14 in. wide and 16 ft. long, dressed and cut to the shape shown in *Figure 2.* Spreaders are cut from 2-in. planks, 10 in. wide and 12 in. long, and placed 6 ft. apart between the board sides and fastened with screws. Cut the ends of the boards so they will fit perfectly and make pointed ends to the pontoons, as shown in *Figure 3,*

and fit in a wedge-shaped piece; paint the joints with durable latex paint and fasten well with screws.

Turn this shell upside down and lay a board ½ in. thick, 12 in. wide and 16 ft. long on the edges of the sides. Mark on the underside the outside line of the shell and cut to shape roughly. See that the spreaders

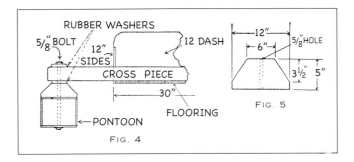

FIG. 5

FIG. 4

and sides fit true all over, then paint the joint and nail with 1¾-in. finishing nails as close as possible without weakening the wood. Slightly stagger the nails in the sides—the 1-in. side boards will allow for this—trim off the sides, turn the box over and paint the joints and ends of the spreaders, giving them two or three coats, and let them dry.

Try each compartment for leaks by turning water in them one at a time. Bore a ⅝-in. hole through each spreader in the center and through the bottom board, as shown. The top board, which is ¼-in. thick, 12 in. wide and 16 ft. long, is put on the same as the bottom.

After finishing both pontoons in this way, place them parallel. A block of wood is fastened on top of each pontoon and exactly over each spreader, on which to bolt the crosspieces, as shown in *Figure 4*. Each

block is cut to the shape and with the dimensions shown in *Figure 5*.

The crosspieces are made from hickory or ash and each piece is 2½ in. thick, 5 in. wide and 6½ ft. long. Bore a ⅝-in. hole 3 in. from each end through the 5-in. way of the wood. Take maple flooring ¾ in. thick, 6 in. wide, 74½ in. long and fasten with large screws and washers to the crosspieces upside down. Fasten to the pontoons with long ⅝-in. bolts put through the spreaders. Put a washer on the head of each bolt and run them through from the underside. Place a thick rubber washer under and on top of each crosspiece at the ends, as shown in *Figure 4*. This will make a rigid yet flexible joint for rough waters. The flooring being placed on the underside of the crosspieces makes it possible to get the sail boom very low. The sides put on and well fastened will greatly

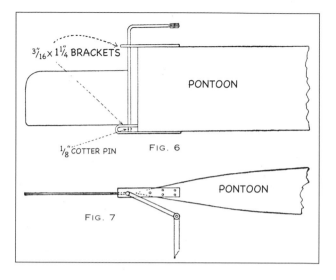

3/16" × 1 1/4" BRACKETS

PONTOON

1/8" COTTER PIN   FIG. 6

PONTOON

FIG. 7

assist in stiffening the platform and help it to stand the racking strains. These sides will also keep the water and spray out, and much more so if a 12-in. dash is put on in front on top of the crosspiece.

The rudders are made as shown in *Figure 6,* by using an iron rod ⅝ in. in diameter and 2 ft. long for the bearing of each. This rod is split with a hacksaw for 7 in. of its length, and a sheet-metal plate ³/₃₂ in. thick, 6 in. wide, and 12 in. long is inserted and riveted in the split. This will allow ¾ in. of the iron rod to project from the bottom edge of the metal, through which a hole is drilled for a cotter pin. The bottom bracket is made from

stake iron bent in the shape of a U, as shown, the rudder bearing passing through a hole drilled in the upper leg and resting on the lower. Slip the top bracket on and then bend the top end of the bearing rod at an angle, as shown in both *Figures 6* and *7.* Connect the two bent ends with a crosspiece which has a hole drilled in its center to fasten a rope as shown in *Figure 1.*

Attach the mast to the front crosspiece, also bowsprit, bracing them both to the pontoons. A set of sails having about 300 sq. ft. of area will be about right for racing. Two sails, main and fore, of about 175 to 200 sq. ft., will be sufficient for cruising.

— HOW TO MAKE A CANOE —

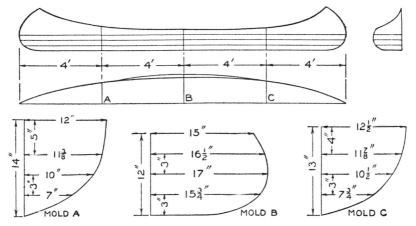

FIG. 1—CANOE AND MOLDS DETAILS.

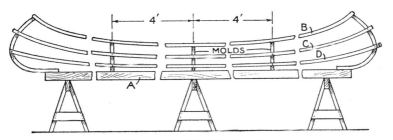

FIG. 2—SHAPING THE CANOE.

A practical and serviceable canoe, one that is inexpensive, can be built by any girl who can wield hammer and saw, by closely following the instructions and drawings given in this article.

It is well to study these carefully before beginning the actual work.

Thus an understanding will be gained of how the parts fit together, and of the way to proceed with the work.

Dimensioned drawings of the canoe and molds are contained in *Figure 1*. The boat is built on a temporary base, *A, Figure 2*, which is a board 14 ft. 1 in. long, 3 in. wide and

1½ in. thick. This base is fastened to the trestles and divided into four sections, the sections on each side of the center being 4 ft. long.

The next thing to be considered are the molds (*Figure 3*). These are made of 1-in. material. Scrap pieces may be found that can be used for these molds. The

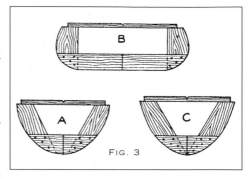

FIG. 3

dimensions given in *Figure 1* are for one-half of each form as shown in *Figure 3,* under their respective letters. The molds are then temporarily attached to the base on the division lines.

Proceed to make the curved ends as shown in *Figure 4.* Two pieces of straight-grained green elm, 32 in. long, 1¾ in. wide and 1 in. thick, will be required. The elm can be obtained from a carriage or blacksmith's shop. The pieces are bent by wrapping a piece of wire around the upper end and baseboard. The joint between the curved piece and the base is temporary. Place a stick between the wires and twist them until the required shape is secured. If the wood does not bend readily, soak it in boiling water. The vertical height and the horizontal length of this bend are shown in *Figure 4.* The twisted wire will give the right curve

and hold the wood in shape until it is dry.

The gunwales are the long pieces, *B, Figure 2,* at the top of the canoe. These are made of strips of ash, 15 ft. long, 1 in. wide and 1 in. thick. Fasten them temporarily to the molds, taking care to have them snugly fit the notches shown. The ends fit over the outside of the stem and stern pieces and are cut to form a sharp point, as shown in *Figure 5.* The ends of the gunwales are fastened permanently to the upper ends of the bent stem and stern pieces with several screws.

Two other light strips, *C* and *D, Figure 2,* are temporarily put in and evenly spaced between the gunwales and the bottom board. These strips are used to give the form to the ribs, and are removed when they have served their purpose.

The ribs are now put in place. They are formed on strips of well-seasoned

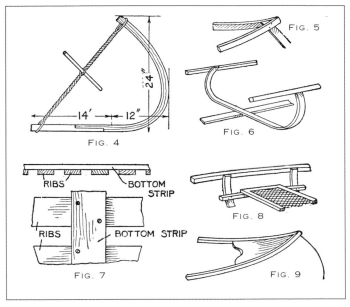

FIG. 5

FIG. 6

FIG. 4

14' 12" 24"

RIBS BOTTOM STRIP

RIBS BOTTOM STRIP

FIG. 8

FIG. 7

FIG. 9

CONSTRUCTION OF THE VARIOUS PARTS.

elm or hickory, soaked in boiling water until they bend without breaking or cracking. Each rib should be 1½ in. wide, ⅜ in. thick and long enough to reach the distance between the gunwales after the bend is made. The ribs are placed 1 in. apart. Begin by placing a rib in the center of the base and on the upper side. Nail it temporarily, yet securely, and then curve the ends and place them inside of the gunwales, as shown in *Figure 6*. Fasten the ends of the rib to the gunwales with 1-in. galvanized brads. This method is used in placing all the ribs. When the ribs are set, remove the pieces *C* and *D*, *Figure 2*, and the molds.

A strip is now put in to take the place of the base. This strip is 1¾ in. wide, ½ in. thick and long enough to reach the entire length of the bottom of the canoe. It is fastened with screws on the inside, as shown in *Figure 7*, and the ends are lap-jointed to the stem and stern pieces, as shown in *Figure 4*. When this piece is fastened in place, the base can be removed.

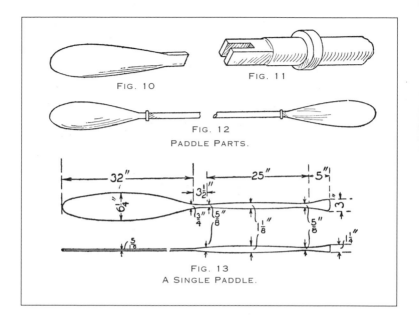

FIG. 10

FIG. 11

FIG. 12

PADDLE PARTS.

FIG. 13

A SINGLE PADDLE.

The seats are attached as shown in *Figure 8,* and the small pieces for each end are fitted as shown in *Figure 9.*

The frame of the canoe is now ready to be covered. This will require 5½ yd. of extra-heavy canvas. Turn the framework of the canoe upside down and place the canvas on it. The center of the canvas is located and tacked to the center strip of the canoe at the points where ribs are attached. Copper tacks should be used. The canvas is then tacked to the ribs, beginning at the center rib and working toward each end, carefully drawing the canvas as tightly as possible and keeping it straight. At the ends the canvas is split in the center and lapped over the bent wood. The surplus canvas is cut off. A thin coat of glue is put on, to shrink the cloth and make it waterproof.

The glue should be powdered and brought into liquid form in a double boiler. A thin coat of this is applied with a paintbrush. A small keel made of a strip of wood is placed on the bottom to protect it when making a landing on sand and stones in shallow water. When the glue is thoroughly dry, the canvas is covered with two coats of durable latex paint. The inside is coated with spar varnish to give it a wood color.

The paddles may be made up in two ways, single or double. The double paddle has a hickory pole, 7 ft. long and 2 in. in diameter, for its center part. The paddle is made as shown in *Figure 10*, of ash or cypress. It is 12 in. long, and 8 in. wide at the widest part. The paddle end fits into a notch cut in the end of the pole (*Figure 11*). A shield is made of a piece of tin or rubber and placed around the pole near the paddle to prevent the water from running to the center as the pole is tipped from side to side. The complete paddle is shown in *Figure 12*. A single paddle is made as shown in *Figure 13*. This is made of ash or any other tough wood. The dimensions given in the sketch are sufficient without a description.

— Anchor for a Canoe or Small Boat —

Small craft, particularly those used for fishing or on streams where a current is encountered, should be provided with an anchor. The illustration gives details for making one that is simple in construction and inexpensive. It weighs about 5 lbs. and is heavy enough for light craft up to 18 ft. long.

The main section was made of a piece of 1½-in. angle iron, 10 in. long. The flukes, or end pieces, were made of sheet iron, 2 in. wide and 8 in. long, bent at a right angle and riveted in place. The straps that hold the link, permitting it to swing freely, were made of band iron. The link was made of an old bicycle crank

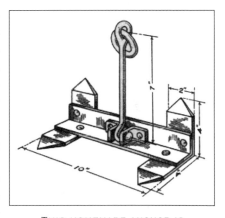

THIS HOMEMADE ANCHOR IS A PRACTICAL ADDITION TO THE EQUIPMENT OF A CANOE OR SMALL BOAT, AND WEIGHS 5 LBS.

into which a ring was forged. It may be made of iron rod, forged into the desired shape and fitted with a ring.

A convenient method of handling the anchor on a boat is to run the line through a pulley at the bow and fasten the end of it to a cleat, near the seat of the person handling the craft. Care must be taken, in a canoe or small boat, that sufficient line is provided to reach the bottom of the anchorage, as otherwise the craft may be overturned.

— ORNAMENTAL FIGUREHEADS FOR THE CANOE —

If you want to be the first in your neighborhood to have something really attractive and novel in the boat line, make some figureheads for the canoe. Figureheads, you may know, were always attached to the prows of old ships as a sort of emblem of good luck. They were carved in beautiful, grained woods, and some that have been preserved in marine museums are genuine works of art. So, just as a good-luck charm, let's see what can be done to decorate the bow of the canoe.

The illustration suggests four different models that can be used and, of course, your personal likes will suggest many more that can be as easily made. If you have no artistic ability, let an artist friend trace out the shape and suggest the coloring. The figure chosen for your decorative scheme must be one that will lend itself to being shaped to fit the curved end of the canoe. Thus the goose, the moose and the bear fit the purpose admirably.

The selected one can be marked out in pencil on the surface of a smooth piece of soft pine, cedar, cypress or any suitable wood, which is easily sawed and whittled. When the outline and details are drawn in, saw out the portions that can be reached with a keyhole saw. Then cut out all smaller details of the edges with a sharp jackknife until the final outline is finished. After that, go over the edges and both sides with fine sandpaper. Draw in the details again with a soft pencil and give the board a coating of shellac. Prime the board with a flat white paint, and when dry, the details can be painted in. As the outlines of the details will show faintly through the priming coat, no redrawing will be found necessary. Use artists' colors if possible and work from a colored print to get the coloring correct. When completed on both sides, set it aside to dry for several days. After the paint has hardened, the surface should be given an application of good spar or automobile varnish. Do not use floor varnish, as this will become white when wet.

Screw a thin strip of oak to the curved part of the back of the figure and let it project 2 or 3 in. at each end. Then, after removing the brass molding from part of the bow, screw the strip in its place. This will support the figurehead in front of and at the top of the bow as illustrated.

— ANCHORS FOR A SMALL BOAT LANDING —

The drawing shows a novel method of using cement blocks to anchor a small boat landing. The blocks are made in a rectangular shape and of a size depending on width of the landing. A block 8 x 8 x 20 in. in dimensions was found to be a convenient size. Lengths of ½ in. flat iron are set into the ends of blocks while the cement is soft, the exposed portion of each piece being rounded to form a ring that fits the pile loosely.

In setting up the framework of the landing, the piles on one side are the first driven in. The rings at one end of the blocks are placed over the piles and the blocks are lowered down to the bottom. The blocks are then shifted to the correct position and the other piles located in the rings and driven down about 2 ft. Crosspieces, nailed to the piles at their upper ends, and two long 2 x 12-in. timbers, nailed along them as shown, form the framework upon which 2-in. lumber is nailed to form a walk. Follow the method outlined above and you'll have a boat landing that is securely anchored and sturdy enough to enjoy for many seasons to come.

CEMENT BLOCKS USED TO ANCHOR SMALL BOAT LANDING. THEY ARE LOCATED BETWEEN THE PILES.

— OLD TIRE RIM SUNK IN GROUND PROVIDES BOAT ANCHORAGE —

Partly buried in the bank of a lake or stream, an old auto tire rim provides a good anchorage for tying up your boat. The rim will last much longer than a wooden post or large stake, and the boat chain cannot be slipped off when it is wrapped once or twice around the rim and locked with a padlock.

— SEWING A SPLIT PADDLE —

The split blade of a paddle or oar can be satisfactorily repaired by the simple process of sewing up the split with copper or brass wire. As a rule such a crack does not extend into the thickest part of the blade and therefore the main consideration is to hold the edges of the crack securely together. To do this, punch or drill a series of small holes all along the crack, on both sides, about ¼ in. from the crack and ½ in. apart. The holes should be staggered, those on one side coming halfway between those on the other side. Clamp or bind the blade so that the crack will be tightly closed, and then sew it together by passing the wire through the holes, beginning at the point farthest from the tip of the blade. When the tip has been reached, work back again, using the same holes. Finish off by twisting the two ends and fastening them down with a copper tack or a small brass screw. Use No. 20 wire,

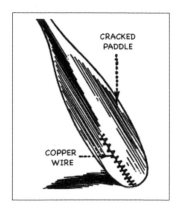

and pull it tight at every stitch. Take care, however, not to break it at the sharp bends. As for the durability of such a repair, an oar repaired in this way has been used for an entire season without having any trouble at the seam. There are, of course, cases where this plan will not work. But in the majority of cases, where the edges are not broken apart on a long taper or bevel, the repair will be effective and permanent.

WALKING *on* WATER

— MAKE YOUR OWN WATER SKIS —

The constantly increasing number of motorboat owners has brought about an equal rise of interest in water sports, among which water skiing is one of the most thrilling. Any craftswoman can make her own

AS YOU RUSH ALONG IN THE WAKE OF A COUPLE OF HUSKY
OUTBOARDS, WATER SKIS GIVE WINGS TO YOUR FLYING FEET.

water skis at less cost than buying them, and will have the added pleasure of building her own equipment.

Spruce is the first choice of wood for the skis, followed by ash, Port Orford cedar and yellow cedar. Whatever wood is used, be sure it is vertical-grained so it will take a smooth bend. If you do not have a jointer, have the lumberyard surface and joint the lumber to a finished dimension of ⅝ x 6 in. and square off both ends. The length of the skis should be determined by the weight of the motorboat used. The table at the end of this article will provide this necessary information. While at the lumberyard, get four lengths

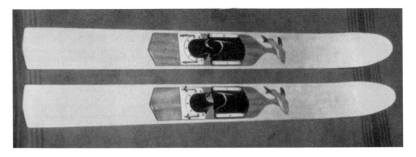

THE "ISLANDS" UNDER THE FOOT BINDINGS OF THESE FINISHED SKIS ARE SHAPES CUT FROM THIN STOCK STAINED DARK.

of ⅝ x ⅝ x 18-in. white oak to be used as the rudders. If oak is not obtainable, the same kind of wood as used for the skis may be used for the rudders. An alternate material for the rudders, depending on personal preference, is 1 x 1-in. aluminum T-bar. The rudders also can be purchased ready-made in some sports stores.

Bending the ski blanks is the first and most difficult step in making the skis, and requires building a bending jig. The jig is built from two 1 x 6s about 6 ft. long. One end of each board is first cut to form the desired radius—20 in. for 5 ft. or less, and 22 in. for 6-ft. skis—and the two 1 x 6s are then joined by cross cleats 14 in. long. The curved section of the jig is either planked solidly with narrow strips, as shown in the detail, or covered with a piece of hardboard to provide a smooth surface.

After the jig is built, the ski blanks must be steamed so they can be bent. The easiest way for the home craftswoman to do this is to set up a 55-gal. oil drum on bricks in the backyard, fill it with water to a depth of 18 in. and build a wood fire under it. The ski blanks are placed in the boiling water and steamed for at least an hour. If the wood is not sufficiently pliable at the end of that time, add more water and boil the blanks longer. When the blanks have been thoroughly steamed, remove them from the water and, holding them side by side, quickly clamp the steamed end over the curved end of the bending jig. Press the opposite ends of the blanks down and hold them with clamps or sandbags. Make sure the straight portion of the skis is parallel to the jig. Use shims and weights or clamps to correct any undesired bends. After the blanks are clamped into place, allow plenty of time to dry and set. One week is the minimum, two weeks are better.

When the blanks are thoroughly dry and set, the next step is to round the front end of each ski. Make a paper pattern, using a 6-in. radius, and then trace the curve on the skis. Cut the curve with a coping, jig or band saw. Now, sand all surfaces and apply three coats of varnish, allowing plenty of time for drying between coats.

The next step is to install the rudders. If wooden rudders are used, they should be shaped to the dimensions given in the detail, sanded and varnished. Use three 1-in. No. 6 brass screws to attach each rudder. Holes must be drilled and countersunk in the aluminum rudders to permit installation. The rudders are located 1 in. from the rear end of the skis and ½ in. from the edges of each ski.

Bindings for the feet are next. They also can be purchased ready-

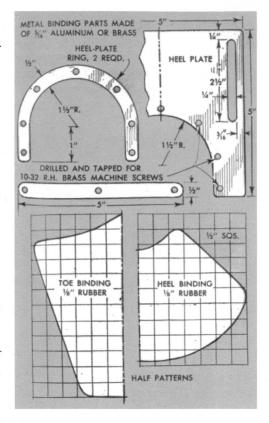

made from a sporting-goods store, but the craftswoman can make them from sheet brass or aluminum which is easily cut and worked with woodworking tools. The rubber used is salvaged from truck inner tubes; the runner is extremely tough and is ⅛ in. thick. The half-patterns for the rubber sections of the heel and toe

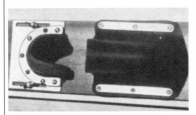

EACH RUDDER IS FASTENED 1 IN. FROM BACK OF SKI AND ½ IN. FROM EDGE. THREE 1-IN. NO. 6 SCREWS ARE USED.

THE TOE SECTION OF THE COMPLETED FOOT BINDINGS IS FASTENED WITH WOOD SCREWS, THE HEEL WITH WING NUTS.

THE ROUNDED FRONT OF THE SKIS IS CUT WITH A COPING SAW AFTER 6-IN. RADIUS HAS BEEN MARKED FROM PATTERN.

AFTER CUTTING THE ROUNDED FRONT END OF THE SKIS, CARE-FULLY SANDPAPER AWAY ALL ROUGHNESS AND SHARP EDGES.

bindings are drawn on ½-in. squares, the paper folded and the completed pattern traced directly on the rubber. The slotted heel plate is drilled and tapped for 10-32 brass machine screws, which are used to hold down the U-shape piece, which, in turn, holds the rubber of the heel binding.

Wing nuts are used on the ¼-in. screws which hold the heel plate to permit adjusting the bindings. The strips for holding the toe bindings are drilled and countersunk to receive brass wood screws.

When installing the bindings, balance the skis on a thin edge to find

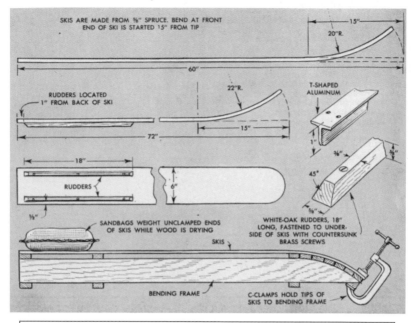

SKIS ARE MADE FROM ⅝" SPRUCE. BEND AT FRONT END OF SKI IS STARTED 15" FROM TIP

15"

20"R.

60"

RUDDERS LOCATED 1" FROM BACK OF SKI

22"R.

T-SHAPED ALUMINUM

72"

15"

1"

⅜"

18"

45"

RUDDERS

6"

½"

SANDBAGS WEIGHT UNCLAMPED ENDS OF SKIS WHILE WOOD IS DRYING

WHITE-OAK RUDDERS, 18" LONG, FASTENED TO UNDER-SIDE OF SKIS WITH COUNTERSUNK BRASS SCREWS

SKIS

BENDING FRAME

C-CLAMPS HOLD TIPS OF SKIS TO BENDING FRAME

TABLE TO DETERMINE LENGTH OF SKIS						
	WEIGHT OF SKIER					
	100–120	140	160	180	200	200 up
10 hp.	4½ ft.	5 ft.	5½ ft.	6 ft.	6 ft.	6 ft.
15 hp.	4½ ft.	4½ ft.	4½ ft.	5 ft.	5½ ft.	5½ ft.
15–30 hp.	4½ ft.	4½ ft.	4½ ft.	4½ ft.	5 ft.	5 ft.
inboards	4½ ft.	4½ ft.	4½ ft.	4½ ft.	4½ ft.	4½ ft.

the exact center of balance. Locate the bindings so the ball of the foot touches directly on this spot.

The "islands" under the foot bindings are simply ornamental wooden shapes cut from thin stock and stained or varnished a contrasting shade. Figures or designs may be carved or jigsawed and fastened to the islands, as shown in the picture of the completed skis on page 135, to give individuality to your skis. If you do use islands on your skis, find the center of balance after they are in place; it is important that the ball of the foot rests on this balance point so that the skis will ride properly in the water.

After the last coat of varnish is completely dry, all you need to try out the product of your labor is a body of fairly calm water and a friend with a motorboat. Use a good, strong tow rope; one can be purchased at a sporting-goods store. If you haven't been on water skis before, take it easy until you get the hang of it. At 30 m.p.h., the surface of the water is a lot harder than it is when you are swimming.

— HOMEMADE LIFE PRESERVER —

Procure an inner tube of a bicycle tire, the closed-end kind, and fold it in four alternate sections, as shown in *Figure 1*. Cut or tear a piece of cloth into strips about ½ in. wide, and knot them together. Fasten this long strip of cloth to the folded tube and weave it alternately in and out, having each run of the cloth about 4 in. apart, until it is bound as shown in *Figure 1*.

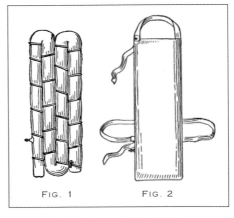

FIG. 1   FIG. 2

INNER TUBE AND COVER.

Make a case of canvas that will snugly fit the folded tube when inflated. The straps that hold the preserver to the body may be made of old suspender straps. They are sewed to the case at one end and fastened at the other with clasps such as used on overall straps. The tube can be easily inflated by blowing into the valve, at the same time holding the valve stem down with the teeth. The finished preserver is shown in *Figure 2*.

— Six Water Skier-to-Tower Signals —

Clear communication between skier and driver is essential for safety when water skiing. Here are six basic signals—from "head that way" to "slow down"—that you should master before strapping on your skis.

OK—Everything's going great.

CUT—I'm going to drop off.

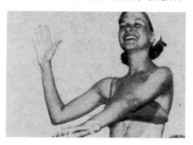

STOP—Let's take a break.

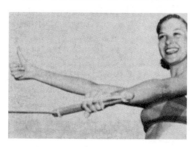

SPEED UP—Pour on the horses.

Head that way.

SLOW DOWN—Take it easy
up there.

— How to Make a Water Bicycle —

FIG. 1—WATER BICYCLE COMPLETE.

Water bicycles always afford fine sport, and, like many another device girls make, can be made of material often cast off by their people as rubbish. The principal material necessary for the construction of a water bicycle is oil barrels. Flour barrels will not do—they are not strong enough, nor can they be made perfectly airtight. The grocer can furnish you with oil barrels at a very small cost, probably let you have them for making a few deliveries for him. Three barrels are required for the water bicycle, although it can be made with but two. *Figure 1* shows the method of arranging the barrels, after the manner of bicycle wheels.

Procure an old bicycle frame and make for it a board platform about 3 ft. wide at the rear end and tapering to about 2 ft. at the front, using cleats to hold the board frame, as shown at the shaded portion *K*. The construction of the barrel part is shown in *Figure 2*. Bore holes in the center of the heads of the two rear barrels and also in the heads of the first barrel. Put a shaft of wood through the rear barrels and one through the front barrel, adjusting the side pieces to the shafts, as indicated.

Next place the platform of the bicycle frame and connections thereon. Going back to *Figure 1*, we see that the driving chain passes from the sprocket driver *L* of the bicycle frame to the place downward between the slits in the platform to the driven sprocket on the shaft between the two barrels. Thus a center drive is made. The rear barrels are fitted with paddles as at *M*, consisting of four pieces of board nailed and cleated about the circumference of the barrels, as shown in *Figure 1*.

The new craft is now ready for a first voyage. To propel it, seat yourself on the bicycle seat, feet on the pedals, just as you would were you on a bicycle out in the street. The steering can be effected by simply bending the body to the right or left, which causes the craft to dip to the inclined side and the affair turns in the dipped direction. The speed is slow at first, but increases as the force is generated and as one becomes familiar with the working of the affair. There

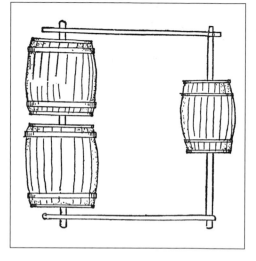

FIG. 2—BARREL FLOAT FOR BICYCLE.

is no danger, as the airtight barrels cannot possibly sink.

Another mode of putting together the set of barrels, using one large one

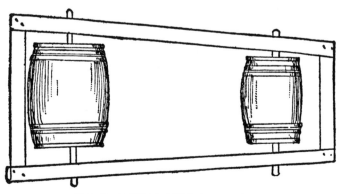

FIG. 3—ANOTHER TYPE OF FLOAT.

in the rear and a small one in the front, is presented in *Figure 3.* These two barrels are empty oil barrels like the others. The head holes are bored and the proper wooden shafts are inserted and the entrance to the bores closed tight by caulking with hemp and putty or clay. The ends of the shafts turn in the wooden frame where the required bores are made to receive the same. If the journals thus made are well oiled, there will not be much friction. Such a frame can be fitted with a platform and a raft to suit one's individual fancy, and then it can be paddled about with ease and safety on any pond. A sail can be rigged up by using a mast and some sheeting; or even a little houseboat, which will give any amount of pleasure, can be built.

CHAPTER 5

THE SPORTING GIRL GETS CHILLY

SLIPPING *and* SLIDING *for* FUN

— "TIP-UP" POLE —

In the north the red-cheeked girl digs a hole in the ice and while she amuses and invigorates herself at skating, the fish underneath the icy sheet fasten themselves to the hook she has let down through a hole. The youngster used to sit over the hole in the ice and wait for the fish to bite, but that became too slow and detracted too much from her

LEFT: "TIP-UP POLE."
RIGHT: "TIP-UP" FISH CAUGHT.

pleasure at skating. So her inventive genius set itself to work and the "tip-up" and "signal" shown in the illustrations was the result. When the fish is not biting, the flag lies flat on the ice, but as soon as a fish has swallowed the hook the flag pole stands straight up wafting its bright-colored flag to the breezes, and all the girls and boys on the skating pond read the word "fish." The fish is drawn up, the hook rebaited, and the youthful fisherman resumes her pleasures on the ice. Often a score or more of these "tip-ups" are planted about the edges of the ice pond, each child bringing her fishing tackle with her skates, and thus finding a double source of amusement. Maybe one youngster will thus have a half dozen different lines in the water at once, it being easy to watch them all together.

The device by which the fish is made to give its own signal when caught is exceedingly simple and any girl can make it. Procure a light rod about 2 ft. in length and to one end fasten a small flag, made of any bright-colored cloth. Bind the rod at right angles to another stick, which is placed across the hole, so that a short piece of the flagrod projects over the cross stick. To this short end fasten the fishing line. Be sure and use strong string in binding the two rods together, and also take care that the cross stick is long enough to permit several inches of each end to rest on the ice. After fastening the line to the short end of the rod, bait the hook with a live minnow or other suitable bait and let it down through the hole. When the fish is hooked the flag will instantly raise and wave about strenuously until the fish is taken from the water.

— "JUMPING-JACK" FISHERMAN —

If the small girl has a "jumping-jack" left over from Christmas, she may make this do her fishing for her and serve as well as the "tip-up," or she can easily make the jumping-jack herself independent of Santa Claus. The string which is pulled to make the joints move is tied securely to the fishing line; the hook is baited and lowered into the water through a hole in the ice. The jumping-jack waves his legs and arms frantically to notify the children when the fish is biting. The jumping-jack is also used for fishing in summertime by placing it on a float which is cast into the water.

"JUMPING-JACK" FISHERMAN.

— MERRY-GO-ROUND WHIRL ON ICE —

A German device for the amusement of children is a whirl on an ice merry-go-round. It is made by placing a vertical shaft or stake, provided with a couple of old cart-wheels, in a hole in the ice. One wheel acts as a turning base and prevents the shaft from sinking into the pond, and the other forms a support for the long sweep attached for propulsion purposes, and should be fastened to the shaft about 3 ft. above the base wheel. The sleds are made fast in a string to the long end of the sweep, which, when turned rapidly, causes the sleds to slide over the ice in a circle at a high speed.

If the sweep is long enough to have each end from the shaft the same length, two strings of sleds may be attached, which will balance the device and make the turning much easier for the child operating the ice merry-go-round.

— THE RUNNING SLEIGH —

Another winter sport, very popular in Sweden, and which has already reached America, is the "running sleigh," shown in the illustration. A light sleigh is equipped with long double runners and is propelled by foot power. The person using the sleigh stands with one foot upon a rest attached to one of the braces connecting the runners and propels the sleigh by pushing backward with the other foot. To steady the body, an upright support is attached to the runners. The contrivance can be used upon hard frozen ground, thin ice and snow-covered surfaces, and under favorable conditions moves with remarkable speed. The "running sleigh" has a decided advantage over skis, because the two foot supports are braced so that they cannot come apart. Any girl or boy can make the sleigh.

— The Winged Skater —

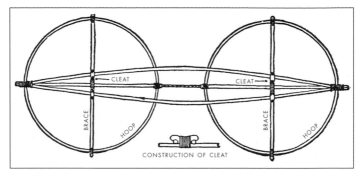

Frame for Skater's Sails.

With the actual speed of the wind a skater may be hurled along the ice if she is aided by sails. She has been known to travel at the rate of 40 m.p.h., and the sport, while affording the limit of excitement, is not attended with danger. The sails are easily made, as the illustrations and description will show.

Secure two large thin hoops about 4 ft. in diameter. They may be obtained from an old hogshead or by bending thin strips. For each hoop select a piece of strong cane about ¾ in. in diameter to constitute the fore and main masts or cross-yards. Extend these across the center of the hoop and fasten each end firmly to the hoop's sides. For the middle of each cross-spar, make a cleat and lash it on firmly. The main spar should also

be made of two pieces of strong cane, each about 9½ ft. long. Bind them together at each end so that the large end of one is fastened to the small end of the other.

Next comes the attaching of the sails to the separate masts. The sails should be made of strong sheeting or thin canvas. Tack the cloth to the hoop on the inner side after it has been wrapped around the hoop two or three times.

Now the main spar should be attached by springing it apart and slipping the cleats of the cross-spar between the two pieces. Bind the inner sides of the hoops tightly together by means of a very strong double cord, as shown in the figure. Then your sail is ready for the ice pond. See that your skates are securely fastened, raise your sail and you will skim along the ice as lightly as a bird on the wing. With a little practice you will learn to tack and guide yourself as desired.

If the hoops cannot be easily obtained, the sails may be made equally effective by using the main spar and fore and main masts as herein described, making the sails square-shaped instead of round and leaving off the hoops. In this case the sails should be securely bound with strong tape. Attach a corner to each end of the cross-spar, and a corner to the outer end of the main spar. The remaining corner of each then appears opposite to each other, and should be fastened together by strong cord in the same manner as the hoops. In this case the sails may be left off until after the frame is

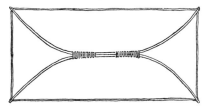

SKATER'S SAIL FINISHED.

entirely put together and then fastened on to the spars by buttons.

A more simple sail may be made according to the plans illustrated in the above drawing. It is made by binding together in the center the halves of two strong hogshead hoops, or two bent poles are better. If possible the sail should be about 8 ft. long and 4 ft. wide. Fasten on the sail at the four corners. The rig will convey two persons and is more easily constructed than any other.

— ICE BOATING —

But the sport that is greatest of all, the one that used to be part of the life of every northern girl or boy, and which is being revived in popularity after years of stagnation, is ice boating. With the aid of old skates, pieces of board and an old sheet or a small bit of canvas, any girl or boy possessed of ordinary mechanical genius may make an

CHILD'S ICE BOAT.

SAIL PLAN

ice boat. The frame of the boat should be made something in the form of a kite. The centerboard should be 4 or 5 ft. long, 6 in. wide and 2 in. thick. The cross board may be of a piece of 1 x 6-in. plank 3 ft. long. Fasten these with braces of small stout strip, as shown in the drawing, and screw the cross-piece securely to the centerboard. Bore a hole in the center of the intersection for the mast pole. The seat may be made of a piece of strong cloth or leather. Three skates are fastened on to either side of the crossboard and one to the rear end of the centerboard, the latter of which is to operate as a rudder. In attaching the skates first make a couple of runner blocks, each 6 in. long and 3 in. wide. Bore holes in them for the straps of the skates to pass through and fasten them securely. Nail the runner blocks firmly to the crossboard about 1½ in. from each end.

In making the rudder, hew down a piece of scantling 1 ft. long until it assumes the shape of a club with a flat base. Nail a strip of wood firmly

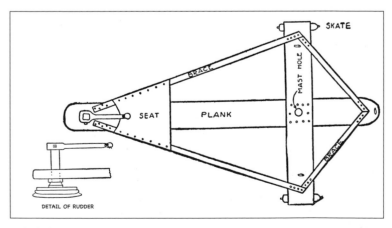

PLAN OF ICE BOAT, SAIL AND RUDDER.

to this base, and to the strip fasten the skate. Run the top of the club through a hole bored in the stern of the centerboard. Then make the helm by boring a hole in one end of a strip of soft board about 1 ft. long, and through this hole pass the club or rubber-pole and fasten it so it may be shifted when desired. Make the sail out of an old sheet, if it be strong enough, piece of canvas, or any such substance, and attach it to the mast and sprit as shown in the illustration, and guide it by a stout string attached to the lower outer corner. As an ice boat will travel faster than the wind, some care and considerable skill is necessary. Unless you are accustomed to managing a sail boat, do not select a place in which to learn where there are air holes or open water. To stop the boat throw the head around into the wind, same as you would with a sail boat. If the wind is strong the occupants of the boat should lie flat on their stomachs. (For more elaborate ice boat plans, see How to Build an Ice-Yacht, page 158).

— THE TOBOGGAN SLED —

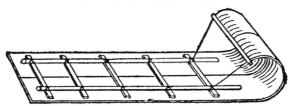

When the snow is very deep a toboggan sled is the thing for real sport. The runners of the ordinary sled break through the crust of the deep snow, blocking the progress and spoiling the fun. The toboggan sled, with its broad, smooth bottom, glides along over the soft surface with perfect ease.

To make the toboggan sled, secure two boards each 10 ft. long and 1 ft. wide and so thin that they can be easily bent. Place the boards beside each other and join them together with cross sticks. Screw the boards to the cross sticks from the bottom and be sure that the heads of the screws are buried deep enough in the wood to not protrude, so that the bottom will present an absolutely smooth surface to the snow. Fasten two side bars to the top of the cross sticks and screw them firmly. In some instances the timbers are fastened together by strings, a groove being cut in the bottom of the boards so as to keep the strings from protruding and being ground to pieces. After the side bars are securely fastened, bend the ends of the boards over and tie them to the ends of the front cross bar to hold them in position, as shown in the illustration. The strings for keeping the boards bent must be very strong. Pieces of stout wire, or a slender steel rod, are even better.

— COASTERS AND CHAIR-SLEIGHS —

Make your own sled, girls! There is no use in buying them because your handmade sled is probably better than any purchased one. There are so many different designs of sleds

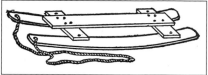

FIG. 1—BARREL STAVE SLED.

that can be made by hand that the matter can be left almost entirely to your own ingenuity. You can make one like the bought sleds and face the runners with pieces of an iron hoop, which will answer every purpose. A good sled for coasting consists simply of two barrel staves and three pieces of board, as shown in the picture, *Figure 1*. No bought sled will equal it for coasting and it is also just the thing for carrying loads of snow for building snow houses. The method of its construction is so simple that no other description is needed than the picture. You can make a chair-sleigh out of this as shown in *Figure 2* by fitting a chair on the cross board instead of the long top board, or it will be still stronger if the top board is allowed

to remain, and then you will have a device that can readily again be transformed into a coasting sled. In making the chair-sleigh, it is necessary, in order to hold the chair in place, to nail four L-shaped blocks on the cross boards, one for each leg of the chair.

FIG. 2—CHAIR-SLEIGH.

— FOLDING CHAIR-SLEIGH —

A folding chair-sleigh is even more enjoyable and convenient than the device just described. If the ice pond is far from home this may be placed under your arm and carried where you like.

Figures 1 and *2* show all the parts as they should look before being joined together. The seat may be made of a piece of canvas or carpet. The hinges are of leather. *Figure 3* shows the folding chair-sleigh after it has been put together. Skates are employed for the runners. The skates may be strapped on or taken off whenever desired. When the chair is lifted the supports

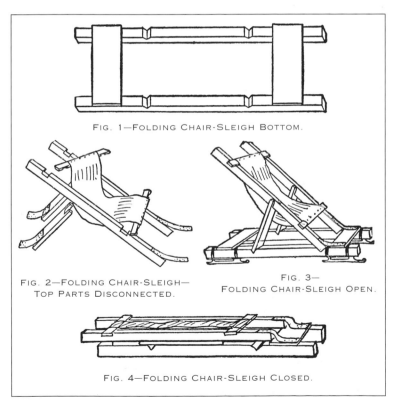

FIG. 1—FOLDING CHAIR-SLEIGH BOTTOM.

FIG. 2—FOLDING CHAIR-SLEIGH—
TOP PARTS DISCONNECTED.

FIG. 3—
FOLDING CHAIR-SLEIGH OPEN.

FIG. 4—FOLDING CHAIR-SLEIGH CLOSED.

slip from the notches on the side bars and fall on the runner bars. The chair is then folded up, as shown in *Figure 4,* so that it can be carried by a child. With regular metal hinges and light timbers a very handsome chair can be constructed that will also afford an ornamental lawn chair for summer.

— THE NORWEGIAN SKI —

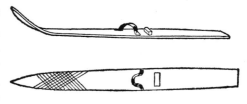

HOMEMADE SKIS.

You have often read of the ski, the snowshoe used by the Norwegians and other people living in the far north. With them the men and women glide down the snow-covered mountainsides, leap across ditches, run races and have all kinds of sport. They are just as amusing to the American child who has ever learned to manipulate them, and it is wonderful how much skill can be attained in their use. Any girl or boy with a little mechanical ingenuity can make a pair of skis (pronounced *skees*). They can be made from two barrel staves. Select staves of straight-grained wood. Sharpen the ends of each and score each end by cutting grooves in the wood, as shown in the illustration. A pocketknife or small gouge will suffice. Then smear the ends of the staves with oil and hold them close to a hot fire until they can be bent so as to tip the toes upward, as shown in the picture. Then with a cord, bind the staves as they are bent and permit them to remain thus tied until they retain the curved form of their own accord. Now screw on top of each ski a little block, just broad and high enough to fit in front of the heels of your shoe. Fasten a strap in front of each block through which to slip your toes, and the skis are made. The inside of the shoe heel should press firmly against the block and the toe be held tightly under the strap. This will keep the skis on your feet. Now procure a stick with which to steer and hunt a snow bank. At first you will afford more amusement to onlookers than to yourself, for the skis have a way of trying to run in opposite directions, crosswise and various ways, but with practice you will soon become expert in their manipulation.

— HAND SLED MADE OF PIPE AND FITTINGS —

The accompanying sketch shows how an ordinary hand sled can be made of ¾-in. pipe and fittings. Each runner is made of one piece of pipe with melted rosin or lead, then bent to the shape desired, and afterward heated to remove the rosin. Each joint is turned up tightly and well pinned or brazed. One of the top crosspieces should have right-hand and left-hand threads or be fitted with a union. Also, one of the top pieces connecting the rear part to the front part of each runner must be fitted to the two crosspieces. Such a hand sled can be made in a few hours' time and, when complete, is much better than a wood sled.

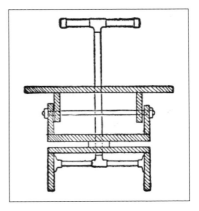

PARTS MADE OF PIPE FITTINGS.

— ROCKER BLOCKS ON COASTER SLEDS —

The accompanying sketch shows a coasting sled with rocker blocks attached on both front and rear runners. The runners and the other parts of the sled are made in the usual way, but instead of fastening the rear runners solid to the top board and the front runners to turn

COASTER SLED WITH ROCKER RUNNERS.

on a solid plane fifth wheel, they are pivoted so each pair of runners will rock when going over bumps.

The illustration will explain this construction without going into detail and giving dimensions for a certain size, as these rocker blocks can be attached to any coaster or toboggan sled. It will be noticed that the top board may bend as much as it will under the load without causing the front ends of the rear runners and the rear ends of the front runners to gouge into the snow or ice.

— ATTACHING RUNNERS TO A BICYCLE FOR WINTER USE —

Instead of storing away your bicycle for the winter, attach runners and use it on the ice. The runners can be made from ¼ x 1-in. iron and fastened to the bicycle frame as shown in the sketch. The tire is removed from the rim of the front wheel and large screws turned into the rim, leaving the greater part of the screw extending. Cut off the heads of the screws and file them to a point. The rear runners should be set so the rim of the wheel will be about ½ in. above the runner level.

BICYCLE FITTED WITH RUNNERS FOR SNOW.

— How to Make Skating Shoes —

Remove the clamp part, as shown in *Figure 1*, from an ordinary clamp skate. Drill holes in the top part of the skate for screws. Purchase a pair of high shoes with heavy soles with screws, as shown in *Figure 2*. When completed, the skating shoes will have the appearance shown on *Figure 3*. These will make as good skating shoes as can be purchased, and very much cheaper.

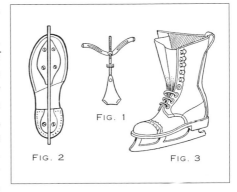

FIG. 1

FIG. 2

FIG. 3

SKATING SHOES.

— Rudder for a Toboggan —

Learning to steer a toboggan by means of the foot dragged behind it is an interesting feature of the sport, but this method is dangerous at times and results in much wear on shoes and clothes. The device shown in the illustration makes this method of steering unnecessary and gives the rider accurate control over the sled. It consists of a strip of ¼ x 1 in. iron curved to form a rudder at one end and twisted at the middle to provide a flat piece for pivoting it on the rear cleat of the sled, as shown in the working drawing. A handle is fastened to the front end of the strip with bolts. The rudder

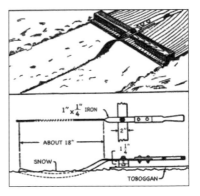

THIS RUDDER FOR A TOBOGGAN ENSURES POSITIVE CONTROL.

should not be curved too deeply or it will cut through the snow and be damaged, or ruin the track.

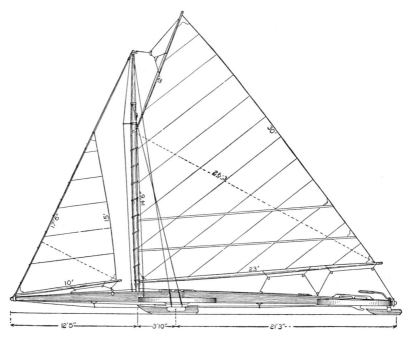

FIG. 1—ICE-YACHT COMPLETE.

— HOW TO BUILD AN ICE-YACHT —

The plans and specifications shown in the illustrations are for making a 400-ft. class yacht, having a double cockpit to accommodate four persons. The weight of the persons in the forward cockpit keeps the boat from rearing when in a stiff breeze. The forward cockpit can be removed if necessary.

The materials used are: backbone, white pine; center, clear spruce; sides, white oak caps; runner plank, bass wood, butternut or oak; cockpit, oak; runners, chocks, etc., quartered white oak. All the ironwork should be first-grade Swedish iron, with the exception of the runners, which are soft cast iron.

It is not necessary to go into detail with the measurements, as they are plainly shown in the sketches. The backbone is 37½ ft. overall, 12 in. in the center, 5 in. stern, 3½ in. at the nose; width 4¼ in. All wood should be selected from the best grades, well seasoned and free from checks. In *Figure 1* is shown the complete ice-yacht with general dimensions for the sail and main parts. Other dimensions are shown in *Figure 2*. The backbone is capped on the upper and lower edges full length with strips of oak, 4¼ in. wide and ⅝ in. thick. The lengthwise side strips of spruce are 1¼ in. thick. The filling-in pieces placed between the side pieces are of seasoned white pine, leaving the open places as shown in *Figure 2*. The parts are put together with hot glue and brass screws.

The runner plank should be placed with the heart of the wood up, so as to give the natural curve from the ice so that it will act as a spring. The plank is 16 in. wide in the center, 14 in. at the ends; 4⅛ in. thick at the center and 2¾ in. at the ends.

Details of the runners are shown in *Figures 3, 4, 5, 6, 7, 8* and *9*. The cast-iron shoes are filed and finished with emery paper, making the angle on the cutting edge 45 deg. on both sides. The runners are 7¼ in. wide overall and 2⅛ in. thick. The soft iron casting is 2¼ in. deep. The shoes are fastened by attaching ⅝-in. machine bolts. These are shown in *Figures 3*

and *9*. The rudder is 2¾ in. thick, 5 in. deep, including wood and iron, and 3 ft. long. The cast-iron shoe is 1⅞ in. deep and fastened on with four ½-in. machine bolts. A brass plate, ¼ in. thick, 2 in. wide and 7 in. long, is inserted on each side of the runners as shown in *Figure 9*. Three holes are drilled through for a ¾-in. riding bolt that can be shifted as desired for rough or smooth ice. The runner chocks and guides are 1⅞ in. thick and 4½ in. deep. They are set in the runner plank ¼ in. and fastened with glue and ½-in. lag screws. These are shown in *Figures 6* and *7*.

The aft cockpit is stationary, while the fore or passenger cockpit can be removed at will. Both cockpits are the same size, 42 in. wide and 7 ft. long overall. Each one has a bent rail, 1½ in. thick and 4 in., grooved ½ in. by ⅞ in. before bending. The flooring is of oak, 1½ in. thick and 4 in. wide, tongue-and-grooved. The forward cockpit is made in halves and hung on the backbone with wrought-iron straps and bolts. These are shown in *Figures 41, 43* and *44*. Two pieces of oak, ½ in. x 4 in., are fastened with screws to the flooring, parallel with the backbone in the forward cockpit. The runner plank which passes under this cockpit gives it stability.

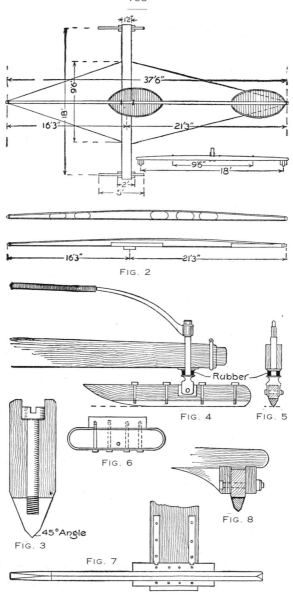

FIG. 2

Rubber

FIG. 4   FIG. 5

FIG. 3   45°Angle

FIG. 6

FIG. 8

FIG. 7

DETAILS OF THE ICE-YACHT PARTS.

The spars should be hollow and have the following dimensions: Mast, 23 ft. 3 in.; heel, 3¾ in.; center, 5¼ in.; tip, 4 in.; boom, 23½ ft.; heel, 3¾ in.; center, 4 in.; tip, 2⅞ in. at ends; gaff, 12½ ft.; center, 3½ in.; ends, 2½ in.; jib-boom, 10½ ft.; 1¾ in. at the ends, 2⅛ in. at the center. The gaff is furnished with bent jaws of oak, *Figure 17,* and the main boom with gooseneck, *Figure 12.*

Galvanized cast-steel yacht rigging, ⁵/₁₆ in. in diameter, is used for the shrouds; jibstay, ⅜ in. in diameter; running plank guys, ⁵/₁₆ in. in diameter; bobstay, ⅜ in. in diameter; martingale stay, ¼ in. in diameter. The throat and peak halyards are ⅜ in. in diameter; jib halyards, ¼ in. in diameter.

The main sheet rigging is ⁹/₁₆-in. Russian bolt rope; jibs, ⁷/₁₆-in. manila bolt rope, 4-strand; jib-sheet, ⅜-in. manila bolt rope. Four ½-in. bronze turnbuckles, *Figure 34,* are used for the shrouds; one ⅝-in. turnbuckle

for the jibstay and one for the bobstay; four ⅜-in. turnbuckles for the runner

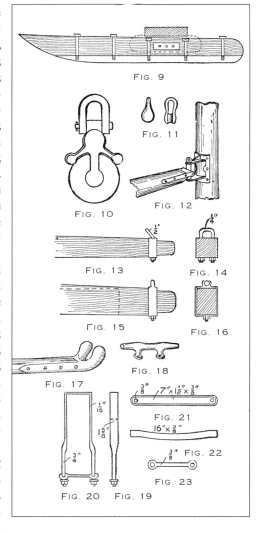

FIG. 9

FIG. 11

FIG. 10

FIG. 12

FIG. 13

FIG. 14

FIG. 15

FIG. 16

FIG. 17

FIG. 18

FIG. 21

FIG. 22

FIG. 23

FIG. 20

FIG. 19

plank stays, and one for the martingale stay.

Two rope blocks for ⅜-in. wire rope, *Figure 10*, are used for the peak and throat, and one block for the wire rope ¼ in. in diameter for the jib halyard. Four 6-in. and one 7-in. cleats, *Figure 18*, are used. The blocks shown in *Figure 11* are used for the main and jib sheets. The steering arrangement is shown in *Figures 4* and *5*. The tiller is 3½ ft. long; rudder post, 1¼ in. in diameter; shoulder to lower end of jaws, 4 in.; depth of jaws, 2⅞ in.; length of post including screw top, 12 in. The rubber washer acts as a spring on rough ice.

In *Figures 13, 14, 15* and *16* are shown metal bands for the nose of the backbone, and *Figures 19, 20, 21, 22* and *23* show the saddles that fit over the backbone and hold the runner plank in place. There are two sets of these. A chock should be sunk in the runner plank at each side to connect with the backbone, to keep it from slipping sidewise as the boat rises in the air. The martingale spreader is shown in *Figures*

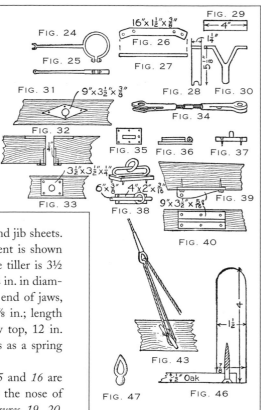

24 and 25. Straps through which the ring bolts for the shrouds pass on the ends to fasten the turnbuckles for the runner plank guys are shown in *Figures 26* and *27*. The bobstay spreaders are shown in *Figures 28, 29* and *30*. In *Figure 31* is shown the top plate for the rudder post and in

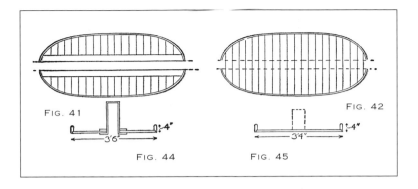

FIG. 41

FIG. 42

FIG. 44

FIG. 45

Figures 32 and *33*, the lower plate for same. The mast step is shown in *Figures 35, 36* and *37*. Two positions of the jib traveler are shown in *Figure 38*. The anchor plate for the bobstay under the cockpit is shown in *Figures 39* and *40*.

At the nose and heel, the runner plank guys end in a loop. The bobstay has a loop at the nose and ends in a turnbuckle that fastens to the anchor plate under the cockpit, aft. The shrouds, jibstay and martingale have loops at the masthead and are spliced bare over solid thimbles. The loops are finished in pigskin and served with soft cotton twine over the splice and varnished. The parceling is done with insulating tape. Serve the tiller with soft cotton twine and ride a second serving over the first. For the halyards hoisting, use a jig shown in *Figure 46*. The

thimble shown in *Figure 47* is made by splicing the rope to the thimble at the running part of the halyard and passing back and forth through cleat and thimble. This gives a quick and strong purchase and does away with cumbersome blocks of the old-fashioned jig. The jib-sheet leads aft to the steering cockpit. The mainsheet ends in a jig of a single block and a single block with becket. Be sure that your sail covers are large enough—the sailmaker always makes them too tight. The cockpit covers must fit tightly around the cockpit rail. Many boats have sail and cockpit covers in one piece.

The woodwork is a matter of personal taste and may be finished as desired by the builder. The dimensions of the sails is a more exact science; these are given in the general drawing, *Figure 1*.

— BOTTLE PUSHERS —

This is a game in which the competitors push bottles on the ice with hockey sticks. All the bottles must be the same size and make. The persons participating must keep their bottles upright at all times. The bottles are lined up for the start and at the word "go," each person pushes a bottle across the field for a distance that is agreed upon.

GETTING COZY

— HOW TO MAKE AN ESKIMO SNOW HOUSE —

Playing in the snow can be raised to a fine art if boys and girls will build their creations with some attempt at architectural skill and not content themselves with mere rough work. Working in snow and ice opens a wide field for an expression of taste and invention, but the construction of houses

LAYING THE SNOW BRICKS.

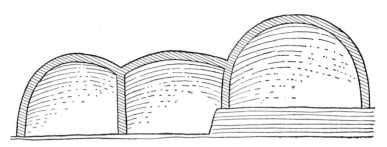

THREE-ROOM SNOW HOUSE.

and forts out of this plastic material provides the greatest amount of pleasure to the normally healthy boy or girl. The snow house makes an excellent playhouse in winter, and represents at the same time a most ingenious employment of the arch system in building. Snow houses are constructed without the aid of any scaffolding or interior falsework, and while there is a keystone at the top of the dome, it is not essential to the support of the walls. These are self-supporting from the time the first snow blocks are put down until the last course is laid.

The snow house is of the beehive shape and the ground plan is that of a circle. The circle is first laid out on the ground and a space cleared for it. Then a row of snow blocks is laid on the ground and another course on top. The snow blocks are not exactly square in shape, but about 12 in. long, 6 in. high and 4 or 5 in. thick.

Larger or smaller blocks can be used, according to the size of the house and thickness of the walls.

First, the snow blocks must be packed and pressed firmly into position out of moist snow that will pack. A very light, dry snow will not pack easily, and it may be necessary to use a little water. If the snow is of the right consistency, there will be no trouble in packing and working with it. As most of the blocks are to be of the same size throughout, it will pay to make a mold for them by forming a box of old boards nailed together, minus the top, and with a movable bottom, or rather no bottom at all. Place the four-sided box on a flat board and ram snow in it, forcing it down closely. Then by lifting the box up and tapping the box from above, the block will drop out. In this way blocks of uniform size are formed, which makes the building simpler and easier.

While one child makes the blocks another can shave them off at the edges and two others can build the house, one inside of the circle and the other outside. Then the door and a window are cut through the wall.

Each layer of snow blocks must have a slight slant at the top toward the center so that the walls will constantly curve inward. This slant at the top is obtained better by slicing off the lower surfaces of each block before putting it in its course. The top will then have a uniform inward slant.

The first course of the snow house should be thicker than the others, and the thickness of the walls gradually decreases toward the top. A wall, however, made of 6-in. blocks throughout, will hold up a snow house perfectly, if its top is no more than 6 or 7 ft. above the ground. If a higher house is needed the walls should be thicker at the base and well up toward the middle.

The builder has no mortar for binding the blocks together, and therefore he must make his joints smooth and even and force in loose snow to fill up the crevices. A little experience will enable one to do this work well, and the construction of the house will proceed rapidly. The Eskimos build additions to their houses by adding various dome-shaped structures to one side, as shown in the illustrations.

A fact not well understood and appreciated is that the Eskimo beehive snow house represents true arch building. It requires no scaffolding in building and it exerts no outward thrust. In the ordinary keystone arch used by builders, a temporary structure must be erected to hold the walls up until the keystone is fitted in position, and the base must be buttressed against an outward thrust. The Eskimo does not have to consider these points. There is no outward thrust, and the top keystone is not necessary to hold the structure up. It is doubtful whether such an arch could be built of brick or stone without scaffolding, but with the snow blocks it is a simple matter.

{ CHAPTER 6 }

TACKLING *the* GREAT OUTDOORS

CAMPING 101

— A HAMMOCK SLEEPING TENT —

Compactness in transportation and general serviceableness are features of the hammock tent shown in the illustration above. It is made by sewing a piece of canvas to the sides of an ordinary "dog," or shelter, tent and may be made of a piece of canvas or tarpaulin. The tent is suspended by the ridge from a heavy rope supported on trees or posts. It is kept taut on the sides by tent ropes attached to stakes driven in the ground.

This form of tent is particularly convenient in providing a good sleeping place in a very small space. Because it is suspended above the ground it is free from dampness, and, with the use of a cot, the camper is provided with a comfortable rest free from prowling animals.

— CAMP SHELTER AFFORDS PROTECTION FROM MOSQUITOS —

When it is undesirable to stay in a camping tent, on warm nights or during the day when a siesta is taken, a mosquito shelter can be made of materials readily available at most camping places. The arrangement, as shown, is made as follows: Procure a number of pliable switches about ¾ in. in diameter and 8 or 10 ft. long—willow or similar growths. Sharpen the butts and force them into the ground in two rows, 3½ ft. apart. Bend the tops together and tie them in arches of the same height, as indicated. Next, tie a ridge binder the entire length. Cover the frame with mosquito netting, providing an entrance at one end.

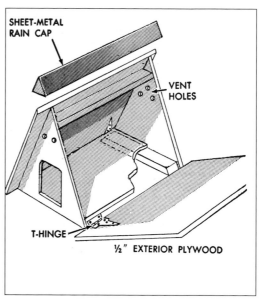

LITHE BRANCHES CUT IN THE WOODS ARE USED FOR FRAMEWORK, WHICH IS COVERED WITH MOSQUITO NETTING.

The shelter shown is for one person but may easily be made larger. The fly, supported on a rope between posts or trees, affords shade.

— How to Make a Folding Canvas Cot —

Instead of sleeping on cold, hard earth when camping, you can construct a relatively comfortable cot. All the materials required to make the cot as shown in *Figure 1* consist of wood 1½ in. square, of which two pieces are 6 ft. long; two pieces 2 ft. 3 in. long; two pieces 2½ ft. long; and four pieces 1½ ft. long; four hinges; some sheet metal and 2¼ yd. of 8-oz. canvas.

Make a rectangle of the two long pieces and the two 2-ft. 3-in. pieces of wood, as shown in *Figure 2,* nailing well the corners together and reinforcing with a strip of sheet metal as shown in *Figure 3.* The four pieces 1½ ft. long are used for the

legs, and two of them are nailed to one of the pieces 2½ ft. long, making a support as shown in *Figure 5.*

Make two of these—one for each end. The hinges are attached as shown in *Figure 5* and the whole support is fastened just under the end pieces of the frame by hinges. Four pieces of sheet metal are cut as shown in *Figure 4* and fastened to the body of the frame with their lower ends hooking over pins driven in each leg at the proper place. The canvas is stretched as tight as possible over the two long side pieces and fastened with large-headed tacks. The legs will fold up as shown by the dotted line and the cot can be stored in a small space.

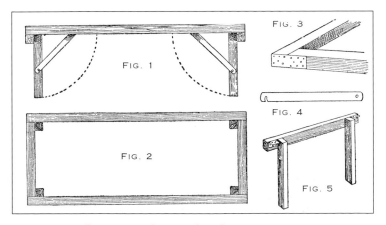

DETAILS OF CANVAS COT CONSTRUCTION.

— A Sheet of Plastic Is Versatile —

A sheet of plastic film has a thousand uses. It'll make a tent or a windbreak or a sunshade, as in *Figure 1*. The plastic will even make a bath or washtub: dig a hole, cover with the sheet and fill 'er up (*Figure 2*).

The same sheet makes a fine raincoat or poncho for sudden showers (*Figure 3*).

Get the heavy-duty dropcloth type; install grommets if you'll be using it for a tent.

FIG. 1

FIG. 2

FIG. 3

— Crotched Stick Driven in Ground Serves as Camp Bootjack —

Campers who wear rubber boots will find that a crotched stick will serve as a bootjack to remove them. Use a strong stick driven into the ground at an angle as indicated in the drawing. A simple tool, it will allow you to yank off your boots without help from a friend or getting your own hands muddy.

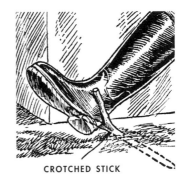

CROTCHED STICK

— Makeshift Camper's Lantern —

While out camping, our only lantern was accidentally smashed beyond repair, and it was necessary to devise something that would take its place. We took an empty tomato can and cut out the tin, 3 in. wide, for a length extending from a point 2 in. below the top to within ¼ in. of the bottom. Each side of the cutout *A* was bent inward in the shape of a letter *S*, in which was placed a piece of glass. Four V-shaped notches were cut, as shown at *B*, near the top of the can, and their points turned outward. A slit was cut in the bottom, shaped

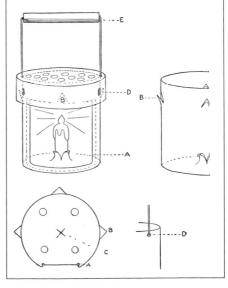

LANTERN MADE OF OLD CANS.

as shown at *C,* and the pointed ends thus formed were turned up to make a place for holding the base of a candle. A larger can was secured and the bottom perforated. This was turned over the top of the other can. A heavy wire was run through the perforations and a short piece of broom handle used to make a bail.

—From a *Popular Mechanics* reader

CAMPFIRE COOKING

— ONE WAY TO COOK A FISH —

One of the best and easiest ways of cooking fish while out camping is shared here by a correspondent of *Forest and Stream.* A fire is built the appropriate size for the amount of food to be cooked, and the wood is allowed to burn down to a glowing mass of coal and ashes. Wash and season your fish well and then wrap them in clean, fresh grass, leaves or bark. Then, after scraping away the greater part of the coals, put the fish among the ashes, cover up with the same, and heap the glowing coals on top. The fish cooks quickly—15 or 20 minutes—according to their size.

If you eat fish or game cooked after this fashion, you will agree that it cannot be beaten by any method known to camp culinary savants. Clay also answers the purpose of protecting the fish or game from the fire if no other material is at hand, and for anything that requires more time for cooking, it makes the best covering. Wet paper will also do the job, especially when you are cooking fish, but clay is king.

— RELIABLE FIRE STARTERS —

Fire starters that burn with intense heat come in handy when firewood is damp. Wrap a kitchen match with yarn, tie it off, and dip it in paraffin. You can make a good supply and carry them in a tobacco tin. Chip the wax off the end to strike.

— Corn Popper Made from Coffee Can and Broom Handle —

With an old coffee can or similar tin receptacle and a piece of a broom handle 2½ or 3 ft. long, it is easy to make a corn popper that is preferable in many ways to a wire one. Take a strip of wood a little shorter than the height of the can to be used and, after boring two holes in it to prevent its splitting, nail it to the end of the handle. The

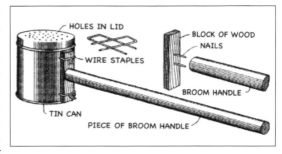

latter is then fastened to the side of the can with two wimples, as shown. Holes are made in the can top to admit air to the corn as it is popping.

— Campers' Water Canteen —

While on a summer's camping trip and using a small tent having a sewed-in floor cloth, a camper experienced some trouble with the water canteen during sultry nights. Sometimes the stopper of the water bottle became dislodged through the unconscious movements of the sleeper, and it was often a problem how to stow this equipment so that there would be no danger of spilling water on the blanket, yet have the water handy. The drawing shows how the problem was solved. The barrel was simply placed outside of the tent and a length of rub-

RUBBER TIRE SUPPLIED CAMPER WITH WATER INSIDE OF TENT FROM OUTSIDE CANTEEN.

ber tubing used as siphon. A leather washer sewed both inside and outside, around the hole in the tent, prevented wear on the canvas.

— SELF-SHARPENING SHEATH —

Your hunting knife or carver will be kept keen-edged and rust free in this abrasive-lined felt sheath. To make it, stitch a piece of fine abrasive cloth between two layers of ⅛-in. felt, sized to fit your blade snugly so that the abrasive will hone the cutting edge each time the blade is inserted or withdrawn. To prevent

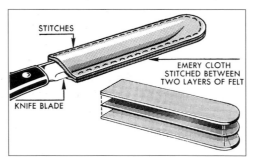

the rust that always threatens to ruin a good blade, oil the felt.

— KEEP YOUR MATCHES DRY —

Keeping a reserve of dry matches is a wise move for every camper. A waterproof container that will float can be fashioned from two used shot shells of different sizes, a 16-gauge to hold the matches and a 12-gauge to slip over it as a cover.

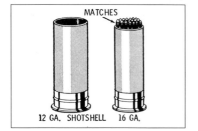

CATCHING *the* BIG ONE

— MAKING ROUND RODS FOR FISHING POLES —

In looking forward to the enjoyment that may be had in the spring, it is good to prepare and overhaul the fishing apparatus. In doing so, it may be necessary to make a joint for the fishing rod. These can be easily cut if they are sized and run throught holes made in a piece of thin metal as follows: Make several holes of the desired sizes in a steel plate and ream them out with a rather dull taper reamer, so as to leave a burr on one side. This burr should be filed down almost level with the surface of the metal, leaving the edges flat and sharp. If a rod of wood from which the article is to be made is put in a hole and drawn through from the opposite side to the burr, a nice round rod will result. As the rod becomes smaller, use a smaller hole until the required diameter is obtained. A saw plate that is not too thin is the proper thing to use for the steel plate. It will be necessary to draw the temper to make the holes, but it is not necessary to retemper it after the holes are made.

— YARDSTICK FOR FISHING BOAT —

Fishing regulations are becoming more stringent every year, and the fisherman or woman is kept busy with his or her ruler to avoid arrest for keeping fish that are under legal length. To simplify matters, some fishermen mark off the lengths of various kinds of fish on their rods. However, a simpler method of measuring the fish is to tack a yardstick along the inside of the boat, near the bottom, marking the length limit of each variety of fish on it. When a fish is caught, it is placed against the measure and it can be seen at a glance whether or not the fish may be kept.

— FISHING WITH AN UMBRELLA —

Make a handy net for catching killifish, one that can be neatly folded and readily carried in a fishing-rod bag, by re-covering an old discarded umbrella frame with mosquito netting.

Although primarily intended for catching "killies" by placing a few cracked clams or mussels in its center and lowering in shallow water not over 2 ft. deep, it can also be used for catching the beautiful silver-banded spearing by baiting with a few pieces of shrimp. Tie the pieces to the frame near the center and suspend the net in deeper water near a sod bank. When codfish and flounders are running, the net, baited with shrimp, can be used from the end of a dock. One must be patient, allowing the net to remain down for some time before drawing it up, but when the fish are present at all, the number taken at one haul will more than make up for the time spent in waiting.

An old umbrella is also very convenient in "bobbing" for eels at night. String a dozen or more worms on strong thread, winding them up into a ball and wrapping the thread well around the mass. Let the ball sink to the bottom and when you feel a bite, draw in the line and shake the eel off into the umbrella, which has previously been hung over the side of the dock.

— DRYING FISHING LINES —

Wet fishing lines rot rapidly; it is therefore not advisable to keep them on the reel, but they should be wound on a drier of some kind. A simple homemade one is shown in the illustration. It consists of a cylindrical paper box such as a large oatmeal box, glued onto an old phonograph record as indicated. A tab with a ring in it is glued to the box at one end to provide a place to fasten the end of the line. Place the record on the phonograph and start the motor; this enables the line to be

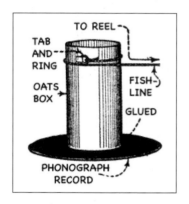

wound from the reel to the box in a very short time without trouble.

— FISHING IN CENTER OF SWIFT RIVER —

How to fish a rushing river in midstream successfully has been a mystery to many who have wanted to try their luck in the far-out pools that are difficult, if not impossible, to reach from shore. For such fishing, the board or trolling guide shown serves excellently.

The device is made from light pine and is 1½ ft. long, 6 in. wide and ¾ in. thick. Both ends are pointed, as shown, the better to cut the water. Four screw eyes are driven into one side of the board. Wires that are stiff enough to prevent bending easily are attached to the eyes, as shown, by making a ring or

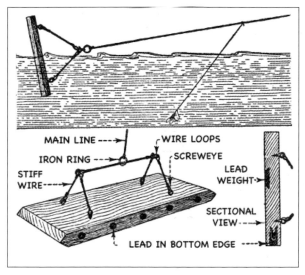

MAIN LINE

IRON RING

STIFF
WIRE

WIRE LOOPS

SCREWEYE

LEAD
WEIGHT

SECTIONAL
VIEW

LEAD IN BOTTOM EDGE

FISHING BLOCK OR TROLLING GUIDE FOR FISHING
IN THE MIDDLE OF SWIFT CHANNEL.

eye at the ends. A horizontal wire with an eye at each end is run between the end wires and is attached to eyes made in the outer ends of the first wires. The line that runs to the boat or fisherman's rod has a ring fastened to it that slides freely along the crosswire. The line with the lure on it is connected to the main line, and with it one can reach the deep spots that cannot otherwise be successfully fished.

To make the block ride the water properly, the bottom edge must be ballasted with lead. Holes are drilled into the edge of the board with an auger bit, a staple or nail driven into

the center of each hold, and melted lead is poured in. Enough holes are made and filled in this manner so that the block will be pulled down in the water to a depth of 3 in. Also, because there is a pull on the line side, this must be balanced by weighing down the opposite side. This can be done by cutting a dovetailed groove along the back of the board and filling it with melted lead, or by fastening a weight to the board above the center. This will make the device swim at the proper angle, so that when there is a pull on the line, the device will not turn over toward the line side.

— Convenient Fly Holder—

A surplus spectacle case of the covered-metal type with a spring-action cover is an ideal holder for those choice flies you keep separate for use as a last resort. Cut stiff cardboard dividers to fit the case curvature snugly, and cement in place.

— How to Wind a Rod —

Here is a chance to own a real fishing rod. All you need is a long piece of bamboo, cut to the length you like. If bamboo is not available, any type of wood that has a certain flexibility will serve the purpose. The principles of winding to make a high-class rod are described simply. Follow each step carefully and take notice of the illustrations.

Although it is somewhat exacting work, anyone with a little patience can learn to wind a rod. Put a spool on a nail and drive the nail into a block of wood. Bend the nail slightly to secure a desired tension and place the spool or spools at your right. Mark the places for guides and in-between winding on the flat or top side of the rod.

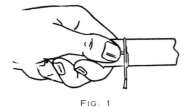

FIG. 1

Hold the rod in the left hand with one end supported between the elbow and body. The right hand is to the left with the loose end extending toward you, *Figure 1*. The portion of the silk extending to the spool should overlap the loose end. Place the tip of a finger where they cross and turn the stick until you see it is going to hold. During the winding the silk must be kept tight, *Figure 2*.

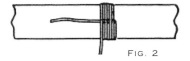

FIG. 2

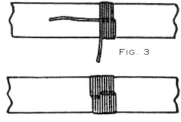

FIG. 3

FIG. 4

After about three complete turns of the rod, take a razor blade or a sharp knife and trim the loose end close to the last turn of the silk. Take this small piece and fold it back against itself, making a loop. Place this between the rod and the thread extending to the spool with the loop end toward you, *Figure 3*. Continue to wind over this loop for at least three turns, then place thumb on the silk to keep it from unwinding, and cut the thread about 2 in. from the rod. Insert the loose end through the loop and pull it back under the winding. Pull the end carefully to be sure the winding is tight, then cut off as close to the silk as possible, in order not to injure the winding, *Figure 4*.

— REPAIRING A FISHING ROD —

Many a broken fishing rod is laid aside because the owner does not know how to repair it properly. The ordinary method of repair is to cut the two ends at an angle and, after applying glue to the surfaces, to join them and wind silk around the joint.

This method can be greatly improved upon by reinforcing the splice with a medium-size darning needle. The sharp end is driven into one piece and the other end is then ground to a point and pushed into the other piece. It may be necessary to drill a small hole in the second piece

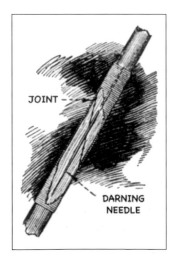

JOINT

DARNING NEEDLE

with a fine drill in order to force the ground point into it without pushing the needle down farther in the first one. The joint is glued and wound with silk. A splice thus made will be the strongest part of the whole rod.

— PENDANT SINKER —

Sly bottom feeders like catfish, some say, won't take bait unless it floats free just above the bottom of the stream. A slight pull on the bait caused by a sinker tied into the line near the bait will cause the wiser lunkers to run after the first nibble. A surer way is to tie a matchstick to the line 8 to 12 in. above the hook and slide a pendant-type sinker down to

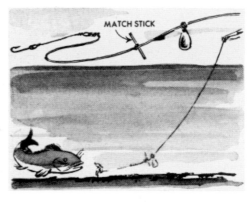

the stick. The sinker can drop to the bottom while bait floats free.

— POCKET HOOK HOLDER —

An assortment of fishhooks can be carried safely in a pocket if you insert the shanks in the center hole of a cork ball fishline float and press barbs into the cork as shown. Since only a small portion of each hook is exposed, there is little chance of dislodging them, as may be a danger when a cylindrically

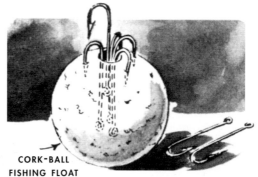

CORK-BALL
FISHING FLOAT

shaped bottle cork is used for this purpose.

— WHISTLE WARNS OF FISH CATCH —

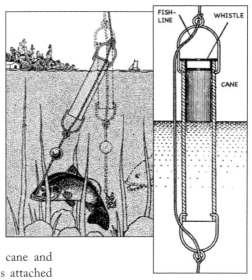

A toy railroad wheel, a piece of hollow can and pieces of wire are the materials necessary for making the whistle shown in the illustration. The whistle warns a fisherwoman that a fish is attempting to make away with her bait. The wheel is fitted into the end of the cane and wedged into place to form a tight joint. The wires are formed into loops at the ends of the cane and fixed to it. The whistle is attached to the fish line, as shown, with the open end down and slightly below the surface of the water. The fishing pole may be fixed so that the whistle will remain in this position while the fisherwoman is at ease in the shade nearby. When the fish attempts to make away with the bait, as shown in the sketch, the water forces the air in the upper part of the cane out through the center hole of the wheel, and a whistling sound is the result.

— MAKE-SHIFT FISH SCALER —

Have fish and no fish scaler? Salvage the lid from a coffee can for the job and you'll find that the sharp edge will lift those scales in a hurry. However, be careful how you hold the lid in order to avoid cutting your hand on this sharp edge.

— Fisherwoman's Personal "Smokehouse" Utilizes Wooden Icebox —

Utilizing an old-fashioned wooden icebox, this "smokehouse" permits a fisherwoman who does not have access to a smokehouse to cure her own catch. The smoke is generated by setting a cast-iron frying pan, filled with maple chips, on an electric hot plate which is placed in the bottom of the icebox. The fish are placed on metal trays on the shelves in the upper section of the box. With both doors closed, a length of 1-in. pipe, set in a hole cut in the top of the box, allows the excess smoke to seep out. Individual tastes will vary, but in the original smokehouse, two hours was sufficient for a good smoking.

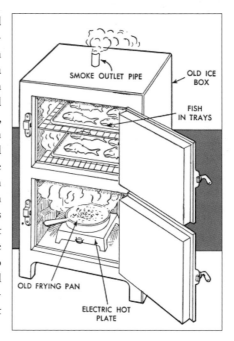

SMOKE OUTLET PIPE

OLD ICE BOX

FISH IN TRAYS

OLD FRYING PAN

ELECTRIC HOT PLATE

— Ingenius Fish Freezer —

To freeze your catch without having to cut the "big ones" down to fit the usual freezer cartons, try quart milk containers. Pack as shown and cover with water to prevent dehydration. For that really big one that didn't get away, use a half-gallon size.

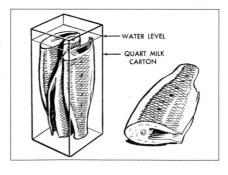

WATER LEVEL

QUART MILK CARTON

— REMOVING FISHHOOKS FROM CLOTHES —

To remove a fishhook from your clothing without damaging the fabric, simply open the eye off the hook with a pocketknife and pull the shank through the cloth, as indicated in the illustrations.

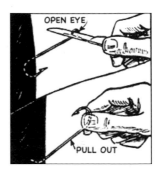

CAMPFIRE CRAFTS MAKE GREAT GIFTS

SURPRISE MOM

— WINTER BOUQUETS —

Dried and sprayed or painted by hand in a riot of colors, common garden flowers and even lowly roadside weeds become a thing of beauty in the form of a winter bouquet.

The best flowers for this purpose are the everlastings, as they are of a papery, strawlike quality and when dried retain their shape and color exceptionally well. These can include

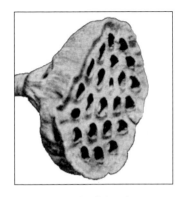

Goldenrod makes a beautiful and lasting bouquet. This was gathered in mid-winter, dried and sprayed with a flat-type paint. You'll find pastel shades give the best results.

Large seed pods of American water lotus and Yoncopin, gilded, can be used to form the predominant part of a winter bouquet when combined with bushy-type grasses.

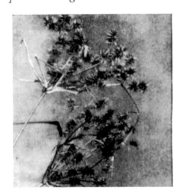

Burr grass, a rough grass, is ideal for winter bouquets. It can be left its natural color and sprayed with clear lacquer to preserve it, or colored by spraying it with paint.

Flowers of the helichrysum plant (strawflowers) when dried retain their shape and colors almost indefinitely. Stems usually are removed and replaced with wire.

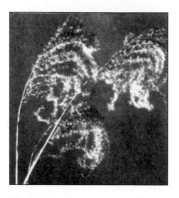

A bouquet combining plume grass with cattails. The grass must be sprayed with thin lacquer to prevent shedding the seed, while the cattails are dipped in collodion.

Here's what plume grass, a cultivated grass, looks like when used by itself in a bouquet. This, like pampas grass, must be sprayed with lacquer to prevent shedding.

Seed pods of a rhododendron bush, when painted with pink or orchid color in contrast with its glossy green leaves, make a striking bouquet to add a decorative touch to a room.

Seed pods entirely make up this bouquet. It combines those of milkweed, wild primrose and mallow. Pods are painted various colors to contrast with green stems.

helichrysum (strawflower), catananche (Cupid's Dart), and winged everlastings. Some others frequently grown in average gardens are sea lavender, globe amaranth and babys'-breath. To prepare everlastings for bouquet material, pick them when the flowers first open from the bud and hang them upside down in small bunches in a warm room, after first stripping off all the leaves. Let them remain until the heat has drawn the last vestige of moisture from the stems. If you wish, the stems can be removed and replaced with ones of wire. Wire stems will permit forming sprays and other unusual arrangements. The bouquet is preserved by spraying it with clear lacquer, which brightens the original colors and gives the bouquet stiffness.

You don't need to stick to flowers alone. Many attractive bouquets can be made up of berries, seed pods and grasses. As for berries, there are those of the bittersweet vine, barberries, Indian currants, coralberries, etc. The hard seed pods of larkspur, primrose, tulip tree and mallow, as well as the globular heads of poppy plants, all lend themselves to forming attractive bouquets. There are also the pods of okra and dried tassels of corn. Roadside weeds, such as the Jimson, milkweed, primrose and many others, are suitable, too. Bouquets of these materials usually are painted with quick-drying paint or enamel, painting the pods in various colors and the stems green.

There are a number of grasses that will do. Plume grass and pampas grass are very good. A variety called sea oats, a tall grass with oatlike panicles, is used commercially. Cattails also are popular in winter bouquets, but like grasses, they have light downy seeds that shed very easily. These can be made nonshedding by coating with collodion cement. Grasses are made nonshedding by spraying them uniformly with thin, clear lacquer or white shellac.

The photos on pages 185–186 show a few of the many seed pods, flowers and weeds that can be used alone or in combination in your arrangements. These photos demonstrate the distinctive and attractive contributions grasses and seed pods can bring to your winter bouquets. An unusual bouquet which is appropriate at Christmas time can be made from a few ordinary tree branches and twigs. These are first painted red or white and then dusted with mica-type artificial snow while the paint is still wet. A rhododendron with its flowerlike seed pods, forms a novel bouquet when the pods are painted pink or orchid and the leaves are green.

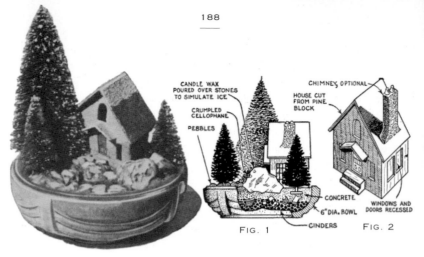

FIG. 1   FIG. 2

— MINIATURE GARDENS IN TRAYS, BOWLS AND WALL NICHES —

Whether it's a fairy house, garden or barnyard scene, or almost any other subject of your own liking, no special artistic talent is necessary to design and make miniature gardens in bowls and trays, which are highly attractive ornaments on wide window sills, in wall niches or on small tables. The plants either may be artificial or they may be real, depending on what is simulated. Other props such as fences, gates, buildings, wells and garden furniture can be made from odds and ends. Small animals, birds and other tiny porcelain figures of correct proportional size can be picked up in the dime or variety store. Small pebbles represent stones and large ones simulate rocks. A little Portland cement mixed with water goes a long way as mortar for building walls, and the use of plaster of paris should not be overlooked.

First of all, you decide where you want to place the tiny garden and how large a base is best. Large, shallow bowls are especially suitable. These should not be less than 2½ in. deep in case you intend to grow some real plants in them, as this space is needed to contain sufficient soil for supplying food and moisture to growing plants. Cover the bottom of the bowl with a ½-in. layer of charcoal and pieces of broken flowerpots, chinaware or stone. This is done to provide a place for excessive water to collect under the soil, because these gardens have no drainage. Then fill the bowl level to the rim or slightly below it with a mixture of rich soil and leaf mold or peat moss. Your florist will do this for you or supply you with the needed materials. The soil should not be pressed down but merely crumbled through the hands when filling.

Figures 1 and *2* show a winter scene in a 6-in. bowl. A layer of cement and sand, mixed with enough water to form "mud," is poured over a layer of cinders. The house, which was cut from a block of wood and painted previously, and also the pine trees, which are simply Christmas ornaments with snow-tipped branches, are set in the soft cement. You can make a small depression to represent a pond or lake,

later painting it blue and gluing a piece of cellophane over it to look like ice. Paraffin, dropped from a lighted candle over the stones and pebbles, looks surprisingly like snow.

The barnyard scene in *Figures 3* and *4* was built on a small wooden base of plywood especially shaped to fit in a wall niche as in *Figure 10*. The fence, gate, well top and barn front were made from ⅛-in. wood available in orange boxes. These, as well as the trees, were glued and bradded to the base. Earth is simulated by a layer of papier-mâché, which can be made by soaking strips of newspaper

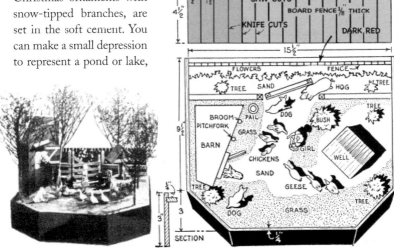

FIG. 3   FIG. 4

to form a pulp, and adding glue. When this has been applied to the plywood, it will stick, and when dry

it is painted with glue on which sand is sprinkled for paths, and sawdust, dyed green, for grass. Various details for a barnyard scene are shown in *Figures 8* and *9*. Note that the head of the horse is glued to a small box which is attached inside of the cut-off barn, just behind the door opening. As the inside is in shadow, the fact that the horse is incomplete will not be noticed. The fencing and well shown in *Figure 9* can be used for other scenes besides the barnyard. A cozy corner in a garden is depicted in *Figure 6*, which includes a garden seat, gate trellis and a gazing ball. Details showing the construction of these parts and their arrangement are given in *Figures 5* and *7*. The gazing ball is a silvered Christmas-tree ball, the neck of which is inserted in plaster of paris, put into the socket of a miniature candlestick. Model airplane cement is ideal for gluing the parts of the gate and other garden furniture. In this case, live plants are used, and the pan, which was used in place of a bowl, was dropped into a large hole cut in a "stage" so that the edge of the pan, painted green, projected just over the edge of the hole. For miniature gardens it is best to select plants that do not require much water. No flowers were used in the model shown. Ferns and small pot plants last longer and require less care. For illumination of a miniature garden placed in a wall niche, a small lamp arranged over the garden, as

shown in *Figure 11*, will set it off to best advantage, a light shield or deflector being provided so that observers do not see the lamp itself.

— USEFUL BASKETS WOVEN FROM RUSTIC MATERIALS —

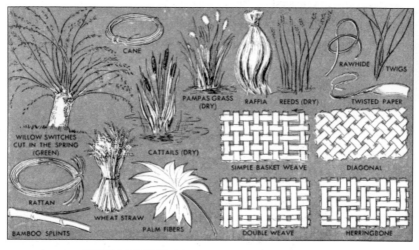

MATERIALS WHICH CAN BE WOVEN INTO BASKETS.

Although it is one of the oldest of the handcrafts, basket weaving is still a popular hobby. Few crafts utilize so many different and inexpensive materials which are readily available almost anywhere. Only a few common hand tools are required: a small handsaw, hammer, drawshave, pliers and pocketknife take care of ordinary requirements.

Among the materials used are green willow twigs or switches, rattan, bamboo splints, wheat straw, dried cattails used flat or twisted, raffia, palm-leaf fibers, thin wood splints such as hickory and basswood, rawhide thongs, cane, twigs, dried reed and pampas grass, tough, twisted paper, and even twine. Most of these are illustrated in the details above. Nearly everyone is familiar with the basic principles of weaving, even though they may not have experience in basketwork. A few examples are shown above. These are the basket weaves done with flat strips, also willow, rattan, rawhide and similar materials adapted to tighter weaving. Several useful baskets of comparatively simple construction are illustrated in *Figure 1*, along with the methods of weaving the different types. Most of this work classes as "under-over" weaving.

As a typical example, an attractive and very handy shopping bag made of dried cattails or rushes is detailed in *Figure 1*. It is finished with a cotton-rope handle bound around with narrow strips of cattail stems. Gather the longest cattail stems you can find and, with a razor blade guided along a straightedge, cut them in 1-in. strips after they have been thoroughly

dried in a shady spot exposed to a breeze. Some of the strips are stained lightly with a brown stain, others left in a natural color to give a two-tone pattern in the finished work. When the cattail strips are thoroughly dry, weave three 38-in. strips into fourteen 29-in. strips in a simple under-over weave as in the lower left-hand detail in *Figure 1*. Then bend up the strips to form sides and weave in horizontal strips until the required height is reached. Some weavers split the vertical strips, *Figure 2*, and tighten the

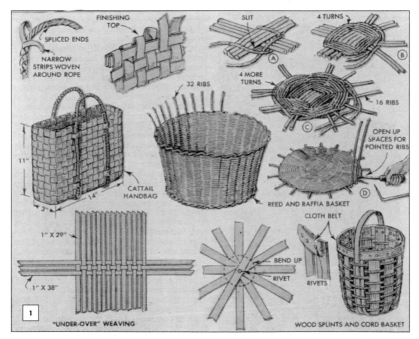

FINISHING TOP

SPLICED ENDS

NARROW STRIPS WOVEN AROUND ROPE

SLIT

4 TURNS

4 MORE TURNS

A

B

32 RIBS

16 RIBS

C

OPEN UP SPACES FOR POINTED RIBS

D

REED AND RAFFIA BASKET

CATTAIL HANDBAG

11"

4"

3"

1" X 29"

1" X 38"

CLOTH BELT

BEND UP

RIVET

RIVETS

1

"UNDER-OVER" WEAVING

WOOD SPLINTS AND CORD BASKET

SPLITTING THE VERTICAL STRIPS.

weave so that the top is smaller than the body of the basket. Before finishing the top edge, note that there are two horizontal strips instead of one. Ends of the vertical strips are turned over and tucked in. A cloth lining, with pockets for purse, letters, etc., will add to the convenience of the bag. The dry cattails will support any load that can be carried easily.

A neat sewing basket, suitable for many other uses, is made as illustrated in the center detail, *Figure 1*. There are two methods of starting the bottom of such a basket, one in *Figure 3*, the other in details *A, B, C* and *D* in *Figure 1*. Employing the latter method, use reed sticks and a bundle of raffia. Cut four of the sticks 6 in. long, and with a sharp knife make slits in each at the center, 1 in. long. Cut four more reeds the same length, sharpen the ends and insert in the slits of the other four as in detail *A*. These are known as spokes and form the base of the basket. Bend the ends slightly downward so that the finished base will be concave and stable on a flat surface. Double a strand of raffia at its center and put it around one of the groups of four spokes, one in front and the other strands behind as in detail *B*. Work around the groups of four spokes in twined weaving four times around. Then separate the spokes into pairs and weave around again four times as in detail *C*. Space all the spokes evenly and continue

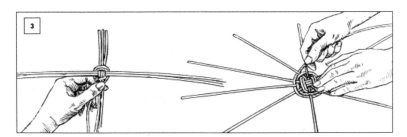

weaving another four turns, making the complete base. Push the raffia toward the center and cut off the ends of the sixteen spokes. With an awl, force an opening between the top and bottom strands, each side of every spoke, and insert sharpened reeds, pushing in as far as they will go, detail *D*. These form the ribs. Pinch the reeds at the base or close to the circular rim of the bottom, and bend up all 32 new ribs. Continue weaving until the wall is finished, leaving about 2 in. of each rib projecting. The top ends of the spokes are bent down and bound in place in the rim.

Another easily made basket suitable for heavier loads is shown in the lower right-hand details of *Figure 1*. Six long, thin wood splints, 2 in. wide, are laid one over another, spoke fashion, riveted in the center and bent up over a large pot lid, wooden disk, or whatever suitable object is handy. Heavy cord or other material is then woven around the upright splints, and the top ends are riveted to the doubled strip of heavy canvas. A rope or splint handle passing entirely around the basket completes the job.

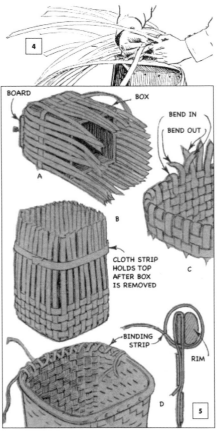

WEAVING WITH WOOD SPLITS.

Still another similar type of basket, heavy and exceptionally strong, is made by beginning with a number of spits woven at right angles over a box slightly smaller than the base area of the basket. Lay the woven splints on top of a box and fasten with a

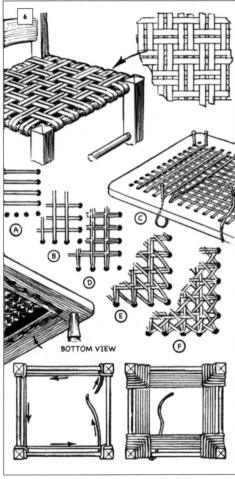

CHAIR CANING.

weaving the walls, carrying these up to a height of three or four splints, as in *Figure 4* and detail *A* of *Figure 5*. Then the box can be removed and the top of the splints held in place by a cloth strip, detail *B*. Next, point the end of each splint, and when the basket is as high as you wish, bend these ends over and tuck them into the horizontal splint which is second or third from the top, as the case requires, detail *C*. Make a rim of hickory, roughly trimmed to a half-round section. Lap and rivet the ends and fasten to the basket top with thin splints bound around in one direction, the other splints bound the other direction, so that they cross as in detail *D*. The ends are tucked under. Some weavers make hickory splints, but usually it is better to buy the splints ready-made.

Woven chair seats can be made from rawhide strips, twisted cattails, cord or rope and the old favorite, cane. A very simple rawhide job is illustrated in the upper

board nailed to the bottom of the box, as shown in *Figure 5, A*. Next, bend the splints down all around and begin details, *Figure 6,* the strips being woven in pairs and the ends tied. Use the longest thongs you can obtain, and moisten them slightly so that they will be taut when dry. Don't soak the thongs, as in drying they may shrink and crack the rungs over which they are stretched.

Cane is commonly used in chair bottoms. A simplified pattern for the beginner is given in *Figure 6.* This is easy to follow and makes a substantial seat. The conventional pattern is carried out in the various steps as shown in *Figure 6,* details *A* to *F* inclusive. Holes are evenly spaced and the cane strip is brought up through a hole, second from the corner, and secured with a tapered wood peg. Front-to-back strips are installed first, detail *A,* and then those at right angles, or crosswise, are completed over the first ones, detail *B.* Again continue with the parallel front-to-back strips and, over these, the second layer of crosswise strips, detail *D,* securing the ends either by tying underneath or driving in a hardwood peg and cutting off the projecting end flush with the chair frame. On the diagonals the work becomes somewhat more complicated. All those running in one direction are installed first. They are followed with the strips running at right angles to the first set of diagonals. See details *E* and *F.* The cane should be soaked a short time before using, but be careful that it is merely damp, not wet. This is quite important in successful weaving.

Rush chair seats are made of dried, twisted cattails and, of course, substitutes are used. If you use cattails, cut them at the peak of growth. Dry them in a dark place and, before twisting, soak in water. Ends of the reeds or stems can be joined in a square knot made only on the underside of the seat. This procedure is shown in the lower details, *Figure 6.* Begin at the corners of the chair frame and work toward the center, twisting the material as you go. Before closing up the seat at the center, pack the empty space between the upper and lower strands with scraps of the same material to make a solid seat.

— THINGS TO MAKE FROM RAFFIA —

Raffia need not be restricted to basket-making alone. You'll find the material suitable for weaving many other useful articles, such as hot-dish pads, attractive overlays for hand bags, coin purses, wastebaskets, etc.

Here are a few examples of what can be done. The wastebasket is made up of fourteen panels of fairly stiff cardboard. Each one is wrapped with raffia as in *Figure 4,* seven of them being covered in black and seven in yellow. Before covering, each strip is scored with a knife ½ in. from one end so that it later may be bent inward easily to form a tab for the bottom. The wrapping is begun at the end opposite

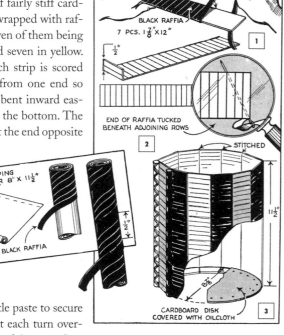

the score, using a little paste to secure the starting end. Let each turn overlap slightly the edge of the preceding one, and when the end is reached, the raffia is pasted and tucked under the winding as in *Figure 2.*

With the tab ends all facing inward, the panels are sewed to one another with black thread, alternating the position of the two colors. The stitches are made through several rows of raffia the full length of the strip, but not through the cardboard. Now paper rolls are made to

SEVEN OF THE FOURTEEN VERTICAL ROLLS ARE FORMED FROM SHEETS OF PAPER 8 X 11½ IN., WHILE THE OTHERS REQUIRE 11½ X 16-IN. PIECES. EACH ONE IS COMPLETELY COVERED WITH RAFFIA AND THEN WRAPPED SPIRALLY WITH A SINGLE STRAND.

cover the seams, as in *Figure 3.* First, sheets of wrapping paper are rolled tightly into a firm roll and pasted along the edge. Seven of these rolls are fully wound with black raffia, after which a single strand of red raffia is wrapped spirally over the black the full length of the roll as in *Figure 4*. The seven other rolls are done in yellow raffia and then wrapped with a double spiral of red—that is, a second strand is wound spirally in a reverse direction from the bottom to the top. In sewing these over each seam of the basket, use small stitches to catch hold of the raffia, and alternate the colors, placing first a black one, then a yellow and so on. Finally, a cardboard disk with black oilcloth glued to the top is sewed to the tabs at the bottom, as shown in *Figure 3*.

The hot-dish mat shown in *Figure 6* may be woven on a piece of common screen wire, or stiff buckram. If the former is used, trim the marginal ends of the wire close to the mesh. First, a double row of stitches about ⅜ in. wide are overcast around the edge of a mat, using a tapestry needle as in *Figure 5*. After this, the center portion is filled in, following the direction of the weave given in *Figure 6*, and finally the finished mat is glued to a felt or cork base, *Figure 7*.

THE MAT IS COMPLETED BY GLUING CORK OR FELT TO THE BOTTOM. CUT THIS SLIGHTLY SMALLER IN SIZE AND PRESS FLAT UNDER A HEAVY OBJECT UNTIL DRY.

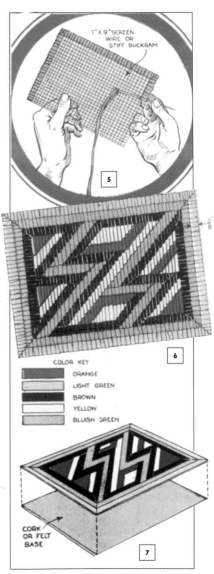

7" X 9" SCREEN WIRE OR STIFF BUCKRAM

5

6

COLOR KEY

ORANGE
LIGHT GREEN
BROWN
YELLOW
BLUISH GREEN

CORK OR FELT BASE

7

MAKING DAD PROUD

— SAILBOAT LAMP HAS RUDDER LIGHT CONTROL —

"Light up" with this novel sailboat lamp means "Port your helm" with the rudder arm and rudder, which controls the toggle switch to turn the light on and off. The light itself is enclosed within a parchment shade, which is shaped around wire frames at top and bottom to resemble a ship's sail.

Most of the construction concerns the hull of the boat. As shown in *Figure 1*, the bottom part of the boat is a separate piece, while the upper part and the cabin are cut from a single thickness of 2-in. stock. By band-sawing the deck line carefully, the cabin will fit into place perfectly. Shaping of the hull sides is accomplished by simply tilting the band-saw table to an angle of 83 deg. A few strokes with a plane will round off the forward sections. After shaping the outside of the hull, the pieces can be taken apart and the necessary cutouts made for the cockpit switch and wires, as shown. It is advisable to make a full-size plan of *Figure 2*, erecting the station lines on 2-in. centers, before commencing the actual construction.

The sail is made from parchment paper, which may be purchased flat or cut from a discarded shade. It is laced around wire loops at the top and the bottom, and then can be laced to the ½-in. dowel which serves as a mast. The jib sail is merely a triangular piece of parchment, cut to the size shown, and suspended on a string running from the mast to the bow of the boat. The boom and the gaff are made easily, and add to the sailboat motif while helping to hold the shade securely in place.

Figure 3 shows the switch detail. This is made by slotting the arm of a small toggle switch so that the brass rudder can be soldered in place. The rudder arm, which is made of ⅛-in. brass, is soldered to the rudder, the whole unit serving as the light switch. The light socket is carried on a ⅛ x 3-in. pipe nipple, which is held to the base of the hull by means of two locknuts. The pipe is cut near the lower end to allow the wires to be connected with the switch.

Additional finishing touches can be added if desired, such as portholes, a small anchor, mooring line, etc. As

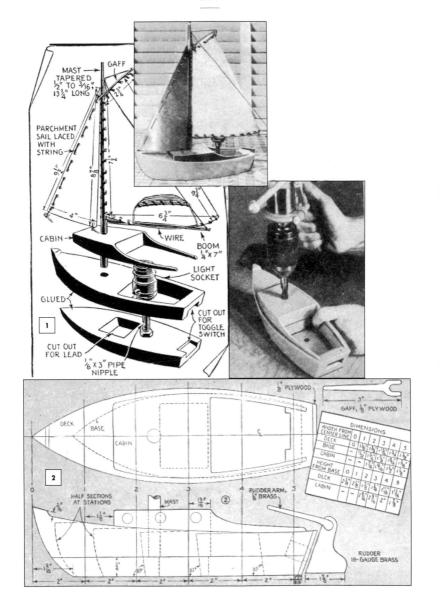

MAST
TAPERED
1/2" TO 3/16"
13 1/4" LONG

GAFF

PARCHMENT
SAIL LACED
WITH
STRING

9 1/2"

8 7/8"

7 1/2"

2 1/4"

4"

9 3/4"

6 3/4"

CABIN

WIRE

BOOM
1/4" X 7"

LIGHT
SOCKET

GLUED

CUT OUT
FOR
TOGGLE
SWITCH

1

CUT OUT
FOR LEAD

1/8" X 3" PIPE
NIPPLE

1/8" PLYWOOD

3"

GAFF, 1/8" PLYWOOD

DECK

BASE

CABIN

C

2

HALF SECTIONS
AT STATIONS

1 3/16"

1 5/8"

MAST

13 3/16"

②

RUDDER ARM,
1/8" BRASS

1 3/8"

2"

2"

2"

2"

2"

1 3/8"

RUDDER
18-GAUGE BRASS

8 3/4"

8 3/4"

8 3/4"

0   1   2   3   4   5

DIMENSIONS						
WIDTH FROM CENTER LINE	0	1	2	3	4	5
DECK	0	1 1/8"	1 5/8"	1 5/8"	1 7/8"	1 13/16"
BASE	—	1 5/8"	1 5/8"	1 5/8"	1 5/16"	1"
CABIN	—	—	1 9/16"	1 5/8"	1 9/16"	—
HEIGHT FROM BASE	0	1	2	3	4	5
DECK	2 3/8"	2 1/8"	1 7/8"	1 5/8"	1 5/8"	1 3/4"
CABIN	—	—	2 1/16"	2"	2"	1 3/8"

shown in the top photo, page 201, the hull is done in white pine with colorful lacquer finish. A varnish finish on hardwood would make up nicely also. The lead weight in the lower part of the hull makes the lamp "stay put," but could be omitted if desired. The bottom should be covered with felt to prevent the wood from marring polished surfaces.

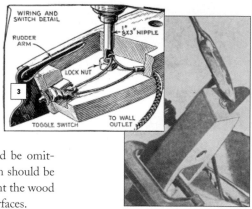

— HOBBIES IN LEATHER: LEATHERCRAFT —

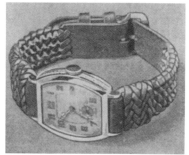

Adapted from the ornate braiding adorning the sword belts of early Spanish conquistadores, these two examples of leatherwork, although seemingly complicated, actually are quite simple and fascinating to braid. The wristwatch band, *Figure 1,* and the belt, *Figure 2,* which is of the same braid, only made wider, are but two of the many practical accessories to which this attractive braid is suited. In addition to the procedure given for braiding

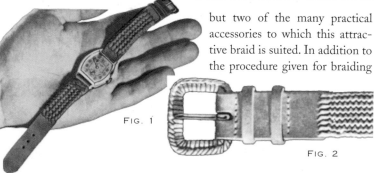

FIG. 1

FIG. 2

a strap or belt, instructions also explain how to braid a Turk's head knot and how to cover a buckle.

The wristwatch band requires a piece of calfskin ⅝ in. wide x 8⅛ in. long, three yards of ⅛-in. beveled goatskin lacing and a buckle with a ⅝-in. opening. For tools, you'll need a knife, a thonging chisel, a leather punch, an awl or fid, a lacing needle and a tube of cellulose cement. The end of the lacing is skived, then inserted in the needle and held with a dab of cement. The calfskin strip is cut into five pieces, as indicated in *Figure 3.* The piece forming the strap end is rounded at one end, punched for the buckle tongue and perforated with four slits. The slits are made with a thonging chisel held at a 45-deg. angle, 1/16 in. in from the end. The buckle end, which is the same length as the strap end, has a slot cut in it. This is made by punching a hole at each end of the slot and

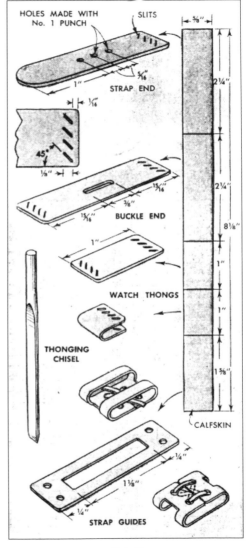

FIG. 3

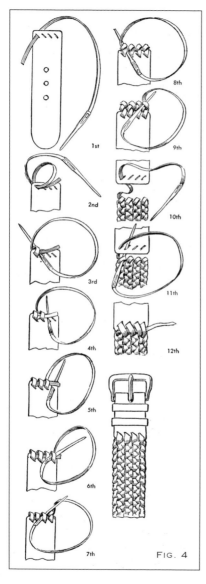

1st

2nd

3rd

4th

5th

6th

7th

8th

9th

10th

11th

12th

FIG. 4

removing the portion between the holes. Aligning slits in each end of the piece are punched at one time while the strip is folded, finished-side out. The two pieces used for the thongs are punched in the same manner. The fifth piece is slotted and folded and the ends are laced together, as shown, to form strap guides.

To braid the wristwatch band, take the strap end and start lacing through the slit at the extreme left, as in *Figure 4,* step 1. Draw the lacing or thong all the way through except for about an inch. Then come back around and go through the same slit again, step 2, drawing the lacing tight. Continuing, the needle is brought forward and pushed through the next slit, step 3, and drawn tight, the end of the thong being underneath. This is repeated as in steps 4 and 5 and then, being sure that the needle passes to the left of the working strand, bring it to the front and pull through the right-hand loop, step 6. Pull it through and tighten and then proceed to come around again and pass through the second loop, step 7, pulling it tight. Keep going back and forth as in steps 8 and 9 until you have about twenty rows braided.

Now, take one of the watch-thong pieces and insert the needle

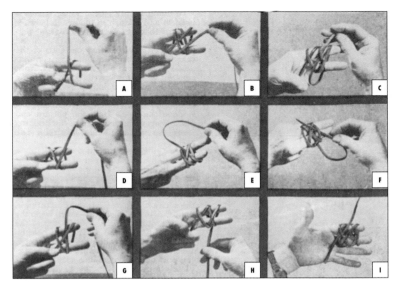

FIG. 5

through the left-hand slit, as in step 10. Then pass the needle through the left-hand loop of the braiding and through the second slit, as in step 11. Proceed in the same way, finishing by bringing the lacing under the loops as in step 12. Cut off the excess and secure the end with a dab of cement. The same procedure is followed in joining and braiding the other parts, but, before attaching the braiding to the other thong, check to see if the band is the right size. In determining the size, remember that the braid when first woven stretches and, therefore, it should be made short enough so it will be fastened by the first hole in the strap.

Braiding a Turk's head knot, which is used to add a finish to the watch band, is done as follows: First make a paper pattern following the diagram in *Figure 5* and form it in a roll so that the ends of the diagram meet and the lines are continuous. Place pins at points marked X. Now, starting where indicated, begin following the lines with the lacing, going around the pins and passing under previous strands at points circled. When finished, remove the work from the pattern and place it over the strap

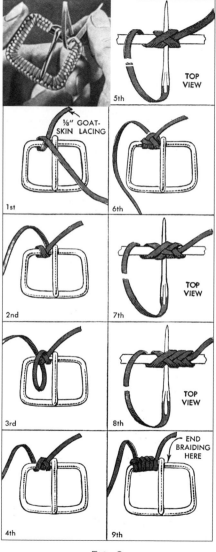

FIG. 6

where the braiding joins the watch thongs. Tighten the Turk's head by gradually taking up the slack, going over the knot several times. When tight, place a drop of cellulose cement between the lacing where the ends meet and cut it off. As you become adept at braiding the Turk's head, it can be formed rapidly on the fingers as shown in the series of progressive steps pictured in photos *A* to *I* inclusive. To start, wrap the lacing around the first two fingers of the left hand as in photo *A*. The part held by the left thumb is called the standing end, the other, the working end. Pass the working part over the standing part and completely around the fingers, as in *B*. Now the working part is passed beneath the standing part, *C*, and around the fingers again. Then continue the working part, inclining it to the extreme right, photo *D*. Note that it passes along the right side of the standing part but, when it reaches the tip of the forefinger, it passes over the standing part and along its left side, passing under the diagonal strand just as the standing part does, photo *E*. Now, bring the working part to the front once more, photo *F*. From this point on, the sequence will be over one strand and under one, leaving the lacing fairly loose, *G*. Working on the back of the hand, photo *H*, the lacing is passed under one of the scallops and over another. Finally, bring the working part alongside the standing part once more, as in photo *I*.

Covering a belt buckle is shown in *Figure 6*. Starting with a yard of ⅛-in. goatskin lacing, and holding the buckle with the heel upward, begin as in step 1. Then pass the lacing around and bring it to the front, as in step 2. Go around again as in steps 3 and 4. Now, closely following the top view, step 5, open the lacing with an awl and insert the needle between the first and second strands, pulling the lacing tight, step 6. Repeat the same procedure, inserting the needle this time between the second and third strands, step 7. Continuing as in step 8, pass the lacing around the buckle, pulling each loop tight to produce the braid shown in step 9. The finished buckle is shown in the photo.

— HOW TO MAKE A LEATHER SPECTACLE CASE —

The spectacle case shown in the accompanying illustration may be made of either calf- or cowskin. The calf skin, being softer, will be easier to work, but will not make as rigid a case as the cowskin. If calf-skin is to be used, secure a piece of modeling calf. The extreme width of the case is 2⅜ in. and the length 6⅝ in. Two pieces will be required of this size. Put on the design before the two parts are sewed together. First draw the design on paper, then prepare the leather. Place the leather on a small non-absorbent surface, such as copper or brass, and moisten the back side with as much water as it will take and still not show on the face side. Turn the leather, lay the design on the face, and hold it in place while both the outline and decoration are traced on the surface with a pencil or some tool that will make a sharp line without tearing the paper.

After the outlines are traced, go over the indentations a second time so as to make them sharp and distinct. There are special modeling tools that can be purchased for this purpose, but a V-shaped nutpick, if smoothed with emery paper so that it will not cut the leather, will do just as well.

Take a stippling tool—if not such tool is at hand, a cup-pointed nail set will do—and stamp the background. It is intended that the full design shall be placed on the back and the same design placed on the front as far as the material will allow. Be careful in stamping not to pound so hard as to cut the leather. A little rubbing on the point with emery will take off the sharpness always found on a new tool. Having prepared the two sides, they may be placed together and sewed around the edges.

If cowhide is preferred, the same method of treatment is used, but a form will need to be made and placed inside the case while the leather is drying to give it the right shape. The form can be made of a stick of wood.

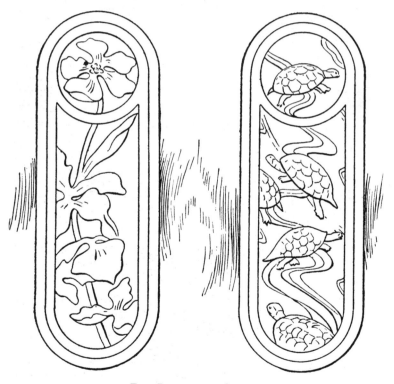

TWO DESIGNS OF CASES.

— CRAFTS FROM THE WOODPILE —

Flower Basket

Tie Holder

Bark-covered tie holders, flower baskets, pipe racks and nut bowls are just a few of the interesting and useful things you can make from materials in the woodpile. The stock is sawed and turned to shape and is then sandpapered smooth before applying shellac for finish. Green wood often splits upon drying out rapidly, so in order to make the wood dry slowly, put the pieces in sawdust, saturate this with water and set away to dry for several months.

Pipe Rack

Nut Bowl

Bank

Novelties

Sewing Set

TREAT YOUR KID SISTER *or* BROTHER

— HUNGRY PELICAN —

Opening and closing his beak in a realistic manner when pushed over the floor, this pelican will delight any small child. Pivoted between jigsawed sides of plywood or hard-pressed board, the upper half of the beak is actuated by a wire connecting rod, which works off a crankpin glued between the wheels which turn on stub axles.

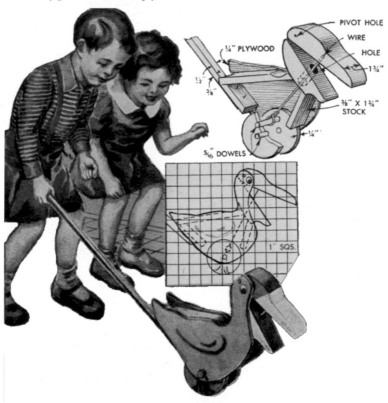

— NIBBLING SQUIRREL —

Like a real squirrel, this one flicks its tail as it nibbles on a nut. Note that the connecting rod is looped over the crankpin to impart a lifelike motion to the tail and front feet. Sand both sides of all the movable parts so that they work freely.

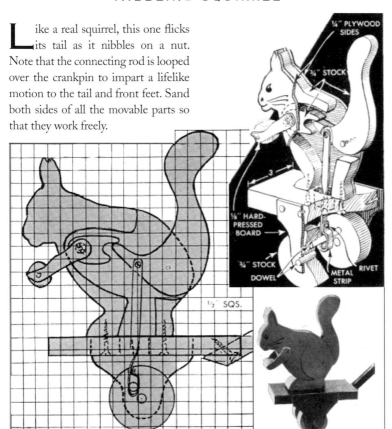

— A JUMPING-FROG TOY —

An entertaining little toy can be made from the wishbone of a fowl after it has been well cleaned and freed from flesh.

Take a piece of strong, thin string and double it, tying it securely to opposite sides of the wishbone about 1 in. from the ends, as in the drawing.

Cut a strip of wood a little shorter than the bone, and make a circular notch about ½ in. from one end. Push the stick through the doubled string for about half its length, twist the string tightly by means of the stick, then pull the stick through until the notch is reached. From a piece of paper or thin cardboard, cut out the outline of a frog. Paint it to resemble the animal as nearly as possible, and paste this to one side of the wishbone. The only material now required is a piece of shoemaker's wax, which is placed on the underside of the bone, just where the free end of the stick will rest.

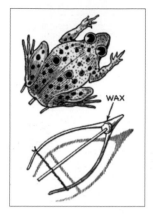

When a child wants to make the frog jump, she only needs to push the

stick down and press the end into the wax. Place the frog on the table, and after a short while the toy will, all of a sudden, make a very lifelike leap as the end of the stick pulls away from the wax.

— TURKEY-HUNT GAME —

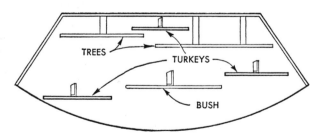

B ag a turkey if you will, but the consequence written on its back may have you scouring the town for a red horsehair or walking upstairs on your hands. The game can be a riot at a party, depending on the originality of the penalties. One turkey wins a prize, but the players don't know which one. The backstop is made of stiff cardboard and painted to represent sky and

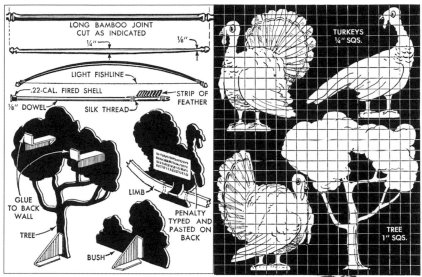

LONG BAMBOO JOINT CUT AS INDICATED

¼"

⅛"

LIGHT FISHLINE

.22-CAL. FIRED SHELL

STRIP OF FEATHER

⅛" DOWEL

SILK THREAD

GLUE TO BACK WALL

TREE

LIMB

PENALTY TYPED AND PASTED ON BACK

BUSH

TURKEYS ¼" SQS.

TREE 1" SQS.

landscape. The trees and turkeys also can be made of cardboard, but they will be more durable if jigsawed from thin plywood. Standards are fitted to the various targets, while tabs permit some of the birds to roost in the trees. A bow is shaped from a piece of bamboo fish pole and strung with a length of fishline. Darts are made of ⅛-in. dowel, tipped with a cartridge shell. Feathers are lashed to the opposite end with silk thread and cement.

INDEX

ALSO AVAILABLE FROM THE EDITORS OF POPULAR MECHANICS

This series celebrates vintage boy- and girlhood with a miscellany of marvelous ideas. From kites, toboggans, and backyard carnivals to science experiments, camping tips, and magic tricks, this collection of projects from *Popular Mechanics'* issues of long ago captures all the appeal of American ingenuity at the start of the last century.

ISBN 978-1-58816-610-4

ISBN 978-1-58816-771-2

ISBN 978-1-58816-754-5

ISBN 978-1-58816-703-3

ISBN 978-1-58816-639-5

ISBN 978-1-58816-509-1

Library of Congress Cataloging-in-Publication Data
The girl mechanic goes outdoors : 160 exciting projects to make and do.
    p. cm.
  Includes index.
  "Popular Mechanics."
  ISBN 978-1-58816-801-6
1. Garden structures—Juvenile literature. I. Popular mechanics (Chicago, Ill. : 1959)
  TH4961.G57 2010
  745.5—dc22

10 9 8 7 6 5 4 3 2 1

Designer: Barbara Balch
Project Editor: Sarah Scheffel

Published by Hearst Books
A division of Sterling Publishing Co., Inc.
387 Park Avenue South, New York, NY 10016

Popular Mechanics is a registered trademark of Hearst Communications, Inc.

www.popularmechanics.com

For information about custom editions, special sales, premium and corporate purchases, please contact Sterling Special Sales Department at 800-805-5489 or specialsales@ sterlingpublishing.com.

Distributed in Canada by Sterling Publishing
c/o Canadian Manda Group, 165 Dufferin Street
Toronto, Ontario, Canada M6K 3H6

Distributed in Australia by Capricorn Link (Australia) Pty. Ltd.
P.O. Box 704, Windsor, NSW 2756 Australia

Manufactured in China

Sterling ISBN 978-1-58816-801-6